SERMONS
for ADVENT *and* CHRISTMAS DAY

SERMONS
for ADVENT *and* CHRISTMAS DAY

MARTIN
LUTHER

HENDRICKSON
PUBLISHERS

Sermons for Advent and Christmas Day

© 2007 Hendrickson Publishers, Inc.
P. O. Box 3473
Peabody, Massachusetts 01961-3473
www.hendrickson.com

ISBN 978-1-61970-981-2

Originally published by Hendrickson Publishers in *Through the Year with Martin Luther*.

Printed in the United States of America

First Printing — July 2017

Cover photo credit: © Exkalibur

Contents

Preface

✦

Martin Luther, 1483–1546

✦

A safe stronghold our God is still,
A trusty shield and weapon;
He'll help us clear from all the ill
That hath us now o'ertaken.
The ancient prince of hell
Hath risen with purpose fell;
Strong mail of craft and power
He weareth in this hour,
On earth is not his fellow.

✦

God's word, for all their craft and force,
One moment will not linger,
But spite of hell, shall have its course;
'Tis written by his finger.
And, though they take our life,
Goods, honour, children, wife,
Yet is their profit small;
These things shall vanish all:
The city of God remaineth.

— *"A Safe Stronghold"* BY MARTIN LUTHER, TRANSLATED
BY THOMAS CARLYLE, 1795–1881

For the modern reader, the long version of Martin Luther's story relies on an unusual vocabulary. A bull? (An official, sealed document issued by the pope.) A diet? (An assembled court of law.) Worms? (A city in Germany.) The Diet of Worms? (Consider the possibilities.)

Martin Luther was born in eastern Germany in 1483. That's some forty years after the German Johann Gutenberg invented a printing press using movable metal type and nearly a decade before Columbus sailed the ocean blue. Having not inherited the family's farm, Luther's father turned to mining and founding metals. Being his father's hope for a son with a secure academic profession, Martin was educated in Latin and then attended the University of Erfurt, receiving a bachelor's and master's in law in 1505.

Martin was a particularly sensitive child, subject to mood swings—highs and lows. Influenced by his region's Germanic, peasantry brand of Christianity, he was haunted by fear—of demons and devils as well as of God the Judge, quick to condemn sinners to interminable punishment. Becoming a monk or priest was considered one sure way of gaining God's favor. For Martin, the decision to enter a monastery came in a July 1505 thunderstorm, when a bolt of lightning knocked him off his feet. On the brink of eternity, he cried out, imploring the aid of Saint Anne: "Help me," and promised, "I will become a monk."

Ordained in an Augustinian order in 1507, he continued educational pursuits, eventually being assigned to the University of Wittenberg to teach moral theology. Young Martin was not a happy man. How could he love God the Judge who was appeased at such a high price? He felt the burden of perfection, including stringent fasting and deprivations that he hoped would "compensate for his sins," to quote Roland Bainton in his acclaimed 1950 biography *Here I Stand*. There was the burden of confession, for scrupulous Martin several hours a day, wracking his brain to find offenses that would potentially separate him from God. There was the financial or physical cost of indulgences; papal bulls decreed that people could buy a proportioned amount of the righteousness of Jesus or a saint and thereby decrease a predeceased loved one's time in purgatory; some bulls went further, offering forgiveness of sin to a living person. Some indulgences were accessible only at churches or shrines containing relics, such as bones of saints. During a 1510 trip to Rome, Martin crawled up the purported (and displaced) steps of Pilate's palace, hopefully praying his grandfather out of purgatory.

After earning a theological doctorate, Martin taught biblical studies at Wittenberg, lecturing principally on the Psalms and then Romans and Galatians. In the writings of Paul, he rediscovered some classical theology of Augustine. Roland Bainton describes what Luther saw in Romans: "It is not that the Son by his sacrifice has placated the irate Father. . . . It is that in some inexplicable way, in the utter desolation of the forsaken Christ, God was able to reconcile the world to himself."

Luther's long-time arguments with, even animosity toward, God withered. He later explained that he had previously taken the phrase "the righteousness of God" to mean "that righteousness whereby God is righteous and deals righteously in punishing the unrighteous." But after much grappling, "I grasped the truth that the righteousness of God is that righteousness whereby, through grace and sheer mercy, he justifies us by faith. Thereupon I felt myself to be reborn and to have gone through open doors into paradise. The whole of Scripture took on a new meaning, and whereas before 'the righteousness of God' had filled me with hate, now it became to me inexpressibly sweet in greater love."

At first Martin thought that his new insight would change the emphasis of his preaching and classroom teaching. But things got complicated. The small university town of Wittenberg was becoming a known center for acclaimed relics and the selling of indulgences. In surrounding areas, some Dominicans were selling even more indulgences, with geographical and cultural implications; German money was being whisked away to Rome to pay for the greatest reliquary of all: Saint Peter's Basilica. This political element helped to fuel the fire that resulted after Martin posted "Ninety-five Theses"—largely against the indulgences industry—in Latin on the door of the Castle Church in Wittenberg on October 31, 1517. If his intent was to engage academic debate, in actuality, he changed the course of the Western church and world.

Translated into German the document was reproduced by an enterprising printer and widely distributed, agitating local peasants. A copy went to Rome. Dominicans took sides against Augustinians. Luther dug in his heels, hitting at the authority of the pope by appealing to the higher authority of Scripture.

By the next summer, like the apostle Paul, Martin was subpoenaed, to appear in Rome, to answer charges of heresy and insubordination. But Luther's local political ruler, Frederick the Wise, had previously assured him that any trial would take place in Germany. A long, three-year tussle—including Luther's claim that the pope was the Antichrist and a papal bull decreeing Luther's excommunication in 1520—resulted in Luther's secular trial, at the Diet of Worms in early 1521.

The Holy Roman emperor himself, Charles V, presided over the trial. First-hand reports quote Martin as holding his ground, refusing to recant, saying, "Here I stand. I can do no other." Found guilty by a depleted number of jurors, Luther might well have been martyred, if not for one friend on the court, Saxony's elector, Frederick the Wise, who organized an abduction, in which Luther was spirited away to a fortress, Wartburg Castle. For about a year in hiding, Luther translated the New Testament from Greek into German, intent on getting the Scriptures into the hands of his people, even though his translation was outlawed by Charles V.

Martin Luther's message spoke freedom for and empowered German's "common man." His early writings (1520) include an *Appeal to the German*

Ruling Class, in which he rallied local rulers to reform the church and protect their people from its extortion and oppression. Here he laid out his understanding of the "priesthood of all believers," in contrast to the prevailing view of the clergy as a caste set apart with special access to God. Here he also proposed that priests be allowed to marry.

The title and contents of another document fueled unrest: *Babylonian Captivity of the Church* (1520) in which he discounted five of seven church sacraments, claiming that only two, Eucharist and Baptism, were biblically instituted. In terms of Eucharist, he insisted that "the cup" to be offered to all believers, not reserved for the clergy only, and he argued against the literalness of transubstantiation—that in the Mass the bread and wine in substance became flesh and blood.

In a third early document (1520), *The Freedom of a Christian,* he explained the tenet of justification by grace through faith alone, not as a result of good works, which were the fruit rather than a contributing source of salvation.

The Diet of Worms decreed that these publications be burned. Many bonfires blazed, but the public had been churned up, and other academics, clerics, and some public officials caught Luther's vision, which opened roads to political as well as spiritual freedom. Priests were marrying. Congregants were sipping Communion wine. The Mass was being said in German. Though it was not part of Martin's "agenda," pictures and statues of the saints were being desecrated. The Wittenberg community was ideologically split, to the point of violence, and in 1522 the city council boldly asked Martin to return to town, in Bainton's view, "probably . . . to exert a moderating influence" in the fray. Cautiously, courageously Martin returned to Wittenberg and indeed he preached "patience, charity, and consideration for the weak. . . . No one can be intimidated into belief." Returning to Wittenberg, Luther was in effect its mayor and priest, leading the town to real reform. Another diet, at Nürnberg, in 1523 revisited charges made at Worms, but a juridical impasse allowed Luther to continue his work, writing, teaching, preaching, leading in circles beyond Wittenberg.

Politics and religion. It's hard for us to understand how intricately intertwined the two were in central Europe in Luther's day. Two publications later that year reflect the scope of Luther's influence. *On Civil Government* was followed by *On the Order of Worship,* an initial attempt at a revised Eucharistic liturgy in which he introduced the idea of congregational singing. In *Christian History* magazine Paul Grime notes, "Music in congregational worship remains one of Luther's most enduring legacies." To fill a gap he'd created, Martin accepted yet another task—that of writing hymns not in Latin but in

German. With ramifications he didn't even understand, Luther was empowering his people. His appeal to all believers to take their stand as equal before God, even to rally in song, contributed to such unrest that by 1525 he was surrounded by a populist uprising known as the Peasants' War. Again he tried to serve as a mediator, writing an *Admonition to Peace,* exhorting the rulers to be less severe and the populace to honor and obedience of secular authority. But when the rebellion didn't subside, Luther sided with the princes (*Against the Robbing and Murdering Horde of Peasants*), advocating a controversially harsh repression.

Into this whirlwind life, and despite some Pauline reservations ("my mind is averse to marriage because I daily expect the death decreed to the heretic"), he brought a bride. Katherina von Bora was a former nun fifteen years younger than himself. Though he married feeling some obligation to provide a home for her, she became a steadying, still point in his life, prompting him eventually to say, "I would not give my Katie for France and Venice together." In red-haired, feisty Katie, Martin had met his match. While Martin was changing the landscape of Europe, Katie was reining him in at home; he was known to call her "my Lord Kate." She had her hands full, managing him, eventually their growing family (six children in all), and their large home (the very Augustinian monastery that Martin had lived in as a young man), which served in effect as a hotel for people passing through or a hostel for the needy and a hospital for the sick, especially in a 1527 plague epidemic that devastated Wittenberg. Some of Luther's best known writings are known as his *Table Talk,* more than 6,500 short discourses he gave to visitors, including disciples, around his dinner table.

One statement about his marriage sheds light back on Martin's public, spiritual persona. "In domestic affairs I defer to Katie. Otherwise, I am led by the Holy Ghost." Luther was sure he spoke for God, though often in exaggerated tones. As he aged his rancor and anger at his enemies is disturbing. He wrote, for instance, "I cannot deny that I am more vehement than I should be. . . . But they assail me and God's Word so atrociously and criminally that . . . these monsters are carrying me beyond the bounds of moderation." The word *Protestant* even then seemed an apt description. That word was first used at the 1529 Diet of Speyer, at which Emperor Charles V again attempted to enforce the Diet of Worms. *Protestant* stuck as a descriptor of the anti-Catholic group(s). Any number of theologians supported Luther in his stand against papal power and extrabiblical traditions and abuses. But as Rome itself headed toward a Counter-Reformation and lost some power in central Europe, Protestant reformers took issue with—even turned on—each other.

Points of doctrine and worship, such as the predestination versus free will, the baptism of infants, the role of music and art, the exact role and meaning of the Lord's Supper, caused rifts among groups of disciples, sometimes along regional lines, notably the Swiss and Dutch disagreeing with the Germans.

The most contentious issue became the "real presence" of Christ in the Eucharistic bread and wine. Though Luther disavowed the Catholic "hocus pocus" of the elements becoming flesh and blood, he appealed to Jesus' "This is my body . . . This is my blood" to counter Ulrich Zwingli's position that Christ's presence in the elements was not real but symbolic and dependent on the faith of the receiver. In 1529 a German prince, Philip of Hesse, persuaded Luther to meet with Ulrich Zwingli and others in Marburg to restore Protestant unity. But there was no compromise and to this day the Reformed and Lutheran traditions are set apart from each other.

Though Luther was making enemies of reformers, he still was in conflict with the Holy Roman Empire. Again under virtual house arrest at a castle fortress, he could not attend a 1530 Diet of Augsburg, at which the Lutheran apologetic, coauthored by Luther and his colleague Philipp Melanchthon, was presented. Professor Eugene Klug of Concordia Theological Seminary notes that for Lutherans, this *Augsburg Confession* became a "standard" for theology, "a document with the weight of a Declaration of Independence."

In midlife Luther was juggling not only matters of state, but also the education of the common man, writing a long and a short version of a *Catechism* that in question and answer format lay out the basics of the faith. The *Small Catechism*, which has been called "the gem of the Reformation," was taught in homes, generation after generation, instilling basic doctrines to the youngest children; it includes phrase-by-phrase explanations of the Ten Commandments, the Apostles' Creed, and the Lord's Prayer. In his spare time, he also continued translating the Old Testament from Hebrew, his complete German Bible being published in 1534.

And, lest we forget, Luther at heart was a teacher and preacher; he left a legacy of more than two thousand sermons, only a portion of those he delivered. The nineteen sermons selected for this volume reflect seasonal themes of the liturgical calendar, the very purpose for which they were written. In 1520, Luther's benefactor, Frederick the Wise, requested that Luther prepare a postil, or sermon, for every Sunday in the church year. His postils were expository studies of the lectionary readings assigned to the Sunday, and were intended to serve as expository guides for other priests, to help them prepare their own preaching. These writings were completed over a period of years and finally became known as the *Church Postils*.

As one would expect, Luther's sermons are grounded in a particular scriptural passage. But from that jumping off point, especially in his later years, Luther slipped in an agenda that not only supported his theological points, but also bitterly denounced groups that disagreed with him, particularly Catholics and also Jews. These tirades against Jews were theological, not racial. (Anthropological distinction between "Aryans" and "Semites" was a nineteenth-century categorization.) His complaint was not that the first-century Jews had killed Jesus, but rather that Jews subsequently did not accept and believe in him. Roland Bainton says, "The supreme sin for him was the persistent rejection of God's revelation of himself in Christ." Where Luther took that line of thought, and how, had drastic consequences in Europe for centuries.

Threads of his disrespect of his contrarians are evident in the sermons in this volume, which should be read for their positive and scriptural insights rather than for their accusative harangues. In his lifetime Luther wrote some 60,000 pages of prose. He welcomed listeners and readers, and yet his deeper desire was that "the Holy Scriptures alone be read." In a similar spirit, may these selected sermons prompt you to search the Scriptures themselves, looking for the basics of Luther's theology, which has been reduced to four points: *sola Scriptura* (Scripture alone being the authority, rather than extraneous tradition), *sola fide* (faith alone, not works, being the channel of our righteousness), *sola gratia* (grace alone—a gift of God—being the cause of our salvation)—all anchored in *solo Christo* (Christ alone). Dr. Timothy George notes that "each *sola* affirmed the centrality of Jesus Christ."

Martin Luther died in 1546, at age sixty-two, after years of continued productivity despite declining health. A year after his death, the emperor declared war on Protestants, set in motion at the Diet of Augsburg. The emperor initially defeated the Protestants, but the tide turned. The 1555 Peace of Augsburg allowed local princes to determine the religion of their districts. This legally recognized Protestantism, though Germany suffered sectarian violence, including the Thirty Years' War, for another century.

Historians feel that early-sixteenth-century Europe was ready for sweeping reform, seeded by John Wycliffe, John Huss, and Desiderius Erasmus, among others. If not Luther it would have been another cleric or academic bridging medieval and Renaissance culture. But it was Martin Luther, a powerful personality, a charismatic motivator, and systematic teacher who shook not just the church but the political world with a basic premise—that we cannot buy or work our way into the kingdom of God.

The First Sunday in Advent

⚜

Faith, Good Works, and the Spiritual Interpretation of This Gospel

And when they drew nigh unto Jerusalem, and came unto Beth-phage, unto the Mount of Olives, then Jesus sent two of his disciples, saying unto them, "Go into the village that is over against you, and straightway ye shall find an ass tied, and a colt with her: loose them, and bring them unto me. And if any one say aught unto you, ye shall say, 'The Lord hath need of them;' and straightway he will send them." Now this is come to pass, that it might be fulfilled which was spoken through the prophet, saying, "Tell ye the daughter of Zion, 'Behold thy King cometh unto thee, meek, and riding upon an ass, and upon a colt the foal of an ass.'" And the disciples went, and did even as Jesus appointed them, and brought the ass, and the colt, and put on them their garments; and he sat thereon. And the most part of the multitude spread their garments in the way; and others cut branches from the trees, and spread them in the way. And the multitudes that went before him, and that followed, cried, saying, "Hosanna to the son of David: Blessed is he that cometh in the name of the Lord; Hosanna in the highest." — MATTHEW 21:1–9

1. In the preface, I said that there are two things to be noted and considered in the Gospel lessons: first, the works of Christ presented to us as a gift and blessing on which our faith is to cling and exercise itself; secondly, the same works offered as an example and model for us to imitate and follow. All the Gospel lessons thus throw light first on faith and then on good works. We will, therefore, consider this Gospel under three heads: speaking first of faith; secondly of good works, and thirdly of the lesson story and its hidden meaning.

I. CONCERNING FAITH

2. This Gospel encourages and demands faith, for it prefigures Christ's coming with grace, whom none may receive or accept save he who believes

him to be the man, and has the mind, as this Gospel portrays in Christ. Nothing but the mercy, tenderness, and kindness of Christ are here shown, and he who so receives and believes on him is saved. He sits not upon a proud steed, an animal of war, nor does he come in great pomp and power, but sitting upon an ass, an animal of peace fit only for burdens and labor and a help to man. He indicates by this that he comes not to frighten man, nor to drive or crush him, but to help him and to carry his burden for him. And although it was the custom of the country to ride on asses and to use horses for war, as the Scriptures often tell us, yet here the object is to show that the entrance of this king shall be meek and lowly.

Again, it also shows the pomp and conduct of the disciples toward Christ who bring the colt to Christ, set him thereon, and spread their garments in the way; also that of the multitude who also spread their garments in the way and cut branches from the trees. They manifested no fear nor terror, but only blessed confidence in him, as one for whom they dared to do such things and who would take it kindly and readily consent to it.

3. Again, he begins his journey and comes to the Mount of Olives to indicate that he comes out of pure mercy. For olive oil in the Scriptures signifies the grace of God that soothes and strengthens the soul as oil soothes and strengthens the body.

4. Thirdly, there is no armor present, no war cry, but songs and praise, rejoicing, and thanksgiving to the Lord.

5. Fourthly, Christ weeps, as Luke 19:41 writes, weeps over Jerusalem because she does not know nor receive such grace; yet he was so grieved at her loss that he did not deal harshly with her.

6. Fifthly, his goodness and mercy are best shown when he quotes the words of the prophets, in Isaiah 62:11 and in Zechariah 9:9, and tenderly invites men to believe and accept Christ, for the fulfilling of which prophecies the events of this Gospel took place and the story was written, as the evangelist himself testifies. We must, therefore, look upon this verse as the chief part of this Gospel, for in it Christ is pictured to us and we are told what we are to believe, and to expect of him, what we are to seek in him, and how we may be benefited by him.

7. First he says, "Tell ye" the daughter of Zion. This is said to the ministry and a new sermon is given them to preach, namely, nothing but what the words following indicate, a right knowledge of Christ. Whoever preaches anything else is a wolf and deceiver. This is one of the verses in which the Gospel is promised of which Paul writes in Romans 1:2; for the Gospel is a sermon from Christ, as he is here placed before us, calling for faith in him.

8. I have often said that there are two kinds of faith. First, a faith in which you indeed believe that Christ is such a man as he is described and proclaimed here and in all the Gospels, but do not believe that he is such a man for you, and are in doubt whether you have any part in him and think, Yes, he is such a man to others, to Peter, Paul, and the blessed saints, but who knows that he is such to me and that I may expect the same from him and may confide in it, as these saints did?

9. Behold, this faith is nothing; it does not receive Christ nor enjoy him, neither can it feel any love and affection for him or from him. It is a faith about Christ and not in or of Christ, a faith which the devils also have as well as evil men. For who is it that does not believe that Christ is a gracious king to the saints? This vain and wicked faith is now taught by the pernicious synagogues of Satan. The universities (Paris and her sister schools), together with the monasteries and all papists, say that this faith is sufficient to make Christians. In this way they virtually deny Christian faith, make heathen and Turks [Muslims] out of Christians, as Saint Peter in 2 Peter 2:1, had foretold: "There shall be false teachers, who shall privily bring in destructive heresies, denying even the Master that bought them."

10. In the second place, he particularly mentions "the daughter of Zion." In these words, he refers to the other, the true faith. For if he commands that the following words concerning Christ be proclaimed, there must be someone to hear, to receive, and to treasure them in firm faith. He does not say, "Tell of the daughter of Zion," as if someone were to believe that she has Christ; but to her you are to say that she is to believe it of herself, and not in any wise doubt that it will be fulfilled as the words declare. That alone can be called Christian faith, which believes without wavering that Christ is the Savior not only to Peter and to the saints but also to you. Your salvation does not depend on the fact that you believe Christ to be the Savior of the godly, but that he is a Savior to you and has become your own.

11. Such a faith will work in you love for Christ and joy in him, and good works will naturally follow. If they do not, faith is surely not present; for where faith is, there the Holy Ghost is and must work love and good works.

12. This faith is condemned by apostate and rebellious Christians, the pope, bishops, priests, monks, and the universities. They call it arrogance to desire to be like the saints. Thereby they fulfill the prophecy of Peter, in 2 Peter 2:2, where he says of these false teachers, "By reason of whom the way of the truth shall be evil spoken of." For this reason, when they hear faith praised, they think love and good works are prohibited. In their great blindness they do not know what faith, love, and good works are. If you would

be a Christian you must permit these words to be spoken to you and hold fast to them and believe without a doubt that you will experience what they say. You must not consider it arrogance that in this you are like the saints, but rather a necessary humility and despair not of God's grace but of your own worthiness. Under penalty of the loss of salvation does God ask for boldness toward his proffered grace. If you do not desire to become holy like the saints, where will you abide? That would be arrogance if you desired to be saved by your own merit and works, as the papists teach. They call that arrogance which is faith, and that faith which is arrogance; poor, miserable, deluded people!

13. If you believe in Christ and in his advent, it is the highest praise and thanks to God to be holy. If you recognize, love, and magnify his grace and work in you, and cast aside and condemn self and the works of self, then are you a Christian. We say, "I believe in the holy Christian Church, the communion of saints." Do you desire to be a part of the holy Christian Church and communion of saints, you must also be holy as she is, yet not of yourself but through Christ alone in whom all are holy.

14. Thirdly he says, "Behold." With this word he rouses us at once from sleep and unbelief as though he had something great, strange, or remarkable to offer, something we have long wished for and now would receive with joy. Such waking up is necessary for the reason that everything that concerns faith is against reason and nature; for example, how can nature and reason comprehend that such a one should be king of Jerusalem who enters in such poverty and humility as to ride upon a borrowed ass? How does such an advent become a great king? But faith is of the nature that it does not judge nor reason by what it sees or feels but by what it hears. It depends upon the Word alone and not on vision or sight. For this reason Christ was received as a king only by the followers of the word of the prophet, by the believers in Christ, by those who judged and received his kingdom not by sight but by the spirit—these are the true daughters of Zion. For it is not possible for those not to be offended in Christ who walk by sight and feeling and do not adhere firmly to the Word.

15. Let us receive first and hold fast this picture in which the nature of faith is placed before us. For as the appearance and object of faith as here presented is contrary to nature and reason, so the same ineffectual and unreasonable appearance is to be found in all articles and instances of faith. It would be no faith if it appeared and acted as faith acts and as the words indicate. It is faith because it does not appear and deport itself as faith and as the words declare.

If Christ had entered in splendor like a king of earth, the appearance and the words would have been according to nature and reason and would have seemed to the eye according to the words, but then there would have been no room for faith. He who believes in Christ must find riches in poverty, honor in dishonor, joy in sorrow, life in death, and hold fast to them in that faith which clings to the Word and expects such things.

16. Fourthly, "Thy king." Here he distinguishes this king from all other kings. It is thy king, he says, who was promised to you, whose own you are, who alone shall direct you, yet in the spirit and not in the body. It is he for whom you have yearned from the beginning, whom the fathers have desired to see, who will deliver you from all that has hitherto burdened, troubled, and held you captive.

Oh, this is a comforting word to a believing heart, for without Christ, man is subjected to many raging tyrants who are not kings but murderers, at whose hands he suffers great misery and fear. These are the devil, the flesh, the world, sin, also the law and eternal death, by all of which the troubled conscience is burdened, is under bondage, and lives in anguish. For where there is sin there is no clear conscience; where there is no clear conscience, there is a life of uncertainty and an unquenchable fear of death and hell in the presence of which no real joy can exist in the heart, as Leviticus 26:36 says, "The sound of a driven leaf shall chase them."

17. Where the heart receives the king with a firm faith, it is secure and does not fear sin, death, hell, nor any other evil; for he well knows and in no wise doubts that this king is the Lord of life and death, of sin and grace, of hell and heaven, and that all things are in his hand. For this reason, he became our king and came down to us that he might deliver us from these tyrants and rule over us himself alone. Therefore, he who is under this king cannot be harmed either by sin, death, hell, Satan, man, or any other creature. As his king lives without sin and is blessed, so must he be kept forever without sin and death in living blessedness.

18. See, such great things are contained in these seemingly unimportant words, "Behold, thy king." Such boundless gifts are brought by this poor and despised king. All this reason does not understand, nor nature comprehend, but faith alone does. Therefore, he is called your king; yours, who are vexed and harassed by sin, Satan, death and hell, the flesh, and the world, so that you may be governed and directed in the grace, in the spirit, in life, in heaven, in God.

With this word, therefore, he demands faith so you may be certain he is such a king to you, has such a kingdom, and has come and is proclaimed for this purpose. If you do not believe this of him, you will never acquire such faith by any work of yours. What you think of him you will have; what you expect of him you will find; and as you believe so shall it be to you. He will still remain what he is, the king of life, of grace, and of salvation, whether he is believed on or not.

19. Fifthly, he "cometh." Without doubt, you do not come to him and bring him to you; he is too high and too far from you. With all your effort, work, and labor you cannot come to him, lest you boast as though you had received him by your own merit and worthiness. No, dear friend, all merit and worthiness is out of the question, and there is nothing but demerit and unworthiness on your side, nothing but grace and mercy on his. The poor and the rich here come together, as Proverbs 22:2 says.

20. By this are condemned all those infamous doctrines of free will, which come from the pope, universities, and monasteries. For all their teaching consists in that we are to begin and lay the first stone. We should by the power of free will first seek God, come to him, run after him, and acquire his grace. Beware, beware of this poison! It is nothing but the doctrine of devils, by which all the world is betrayed. Before you can cry to God and seek him, God must come to you and must have found you, as Paul says, in Romans 10:14–15, "How then shall they call on him in whom they have not believed? and how shall they believe in him whom they have not heard? and how shall they hear without a preacher, and how shall they preach except they be sent?" God must lay the first stone and begin with you, if you are to seek him and pray to him. He is present when you begin to seek. If he were not, you could not accomplish anything but mere sin, and the greater the sin, the greater and holier the work you will attempt, and you will become a hardened hypocrite.

21. You ask, How shall we begin to be godly and what shall we do that God may begin his work in us? Answer: Do you not understand, it is not for you to work or to begin to be godly, as little as it is to further and complete it. Everything that you begin is in and remains sin, though it shines ever so brightly; you cannot do anything but sin, do what you will. Hence the teaching of all the schools and monasteries is misleading, when they teach man to begin to pray and do good works, to found something, to give, to sing, to become spiritual and thereby to seek God's grace.

22. You say, however, Then I must sin from necessity, if by my free will I work and live without God? and, I could not avoid sin, no matter what I would do? Answer: Truly, it is so, that you must remain in sin, do what you will, and that everything is sin you do alone out of your own free will. For if out of your own free will you might avoid sin and do that which pleases God, what need would you have of Christ? He would be a fool to shed his blood for your

sin, if you yourself were so free and able to do aught that is not sin. From this, you learn how the universities and monasteries with their teachings of free will and good works, do nothing else but darken the truth of God so that we know not what Christ is, what we are and what our condition is. They lead the whole world with them into the abyss of hell, and it is indeed time that we eradicate from the earth all chapters and monasteries.

23. Learn then from this Gospel what takes place when God begins to make us godly, and what the first step is in becoming godly. There is no other beginning than that your king comes to you and begins to work in you. It is done in this way: The Gospel must be the first, this must be preached and heard. In it you hear and learn how all your works count for nothing before God and that everything is sinful that you work and do. Your king must first be in you and rule you. Behold, here is the beginning of your salvation; you relinquish your works and despair of yourself, because you hear and see that all you do is sin and amounts to nothing, as the Gospel tells you, and you receive your king in faith, cling to him, implore his grace, and find consolation in his mercy alone.

But when you hear and accept this it is not your power, but God's grace, that renders the Gospel fruitful in you, so that you believe that you and your works are nothing. For you see how few there are who accept it, so that Christ weeps over Jerusalem and, as now the papists are doing, not only refuse it, but condemn such doctrine, for they will not have all their works to be sin, they desire to lay the first stone and rage and fume against the Gospel.

24. Again, it is not by virtue of your power or your merit that the Gospel is preached and your king comes. God must send him out of pure grace. Hence not greater wrath of God exists than where he does not send the Gospel; there is only sin, error, and darkness, there man may do what he will. Again, there is no greater grace than where he sends his Gospel, for there must be grace and mercy in its train, even if not all, perhaps only a few, receive it. Thus the pope's government is the most terrible wrath of God, so that Peter calls them the children of execration, for they teach no Gospel, but mere human doctrine of their own works as we, alas, see in all the chapters, monasteries, and schools.

25. This is what is meant by "Thy king cometh." You do not seek him, but he seeks you. You do not find him, he finds you. For the preachers come from him, not from you; their sermons come from him, not from you; your faith comes from him, not from you; everything that faith works in you comes from him, not from you; and where he does not come, you remain outside; and where there is no Gospel there is no God, but only sin and damnation,

free will may do, suffer, work, and live as it may and can. Therefore you should not ask, where to begin to be godly; there is no beginning, except where the king enters and is proclaimed.

26. Sixthly, he cometh "unto thee." Thee, thee, what does this mean? Is it not enough that he is your king? If he is yours how can he say, he comes to you? All this is stated by the prophet to present Christ in an endearing way and invite to faith. It is not enough that Christ saves us from the rule and tyranny of sin, death, and hell, and becomes our king, but he offers himself to us for our possession, that whatever he is and has may be ours, as Saint Paul writes, in Romans 8:32, "He that spared not his own Son, but delivered him up for us all, how shall he not also with him freely give us all things?"

27. Hence the daughter of Zion has twofold gifts from Christ. The first is faith and the Holy Spirit in the heart, by which she becomes pure and free from sin. The other is Christ himself, that she may glory in the blessings given by Christ, as though everything Christ is and has were her own, and that she may rely upon Christ as upon her own heritage. Of this Saint Paul speaks, in Romans 8:34, "Christ maketh intercession for us." If he makes intercession for us he will receive us and we will receive him as our Lord. And 1 Corinthians 1:30 says, "Christ was made unto us wisdom from God, and righteousness and sanctification, and redemption." Of the twofold gifts Isaiah speaks in 40:1–2, "Comfort ye, comfort ye my people, saith your God. Speak ye comfortably to Jerusalem; and cry unto her, that her warfare is accomplished, that her iniquity is pardoned, for she hath received of Jehovah's hand double for all her sins."

Behold, this means that he comes to you, for your welfare, as your own; in that he is your king, you receive grace from him into your heart, so that he delivers you from sin and death, and thus becomes your king and you his subject. In coming to you he becomes your own, so that you partake of his treasures, as a bride, by the jewelry the bridegroom puts on her, becomes partner of his possessions. Oh, this is a joyful, comforting form of speech! Who would despair and be afraid of death and hell if he believes in these words and wins Christ as his own?

28. Seventhly, "Meek." This word is to be especially noticed, and it comforts the sin-burdened conscience. Sin naturally makes a timid conscience, which fears God and flees, as Adam did in paradise, and cannot endure the coming of God, the knowing and feeling that God is an enemy of sin and severely punishes it. Hence it flees and is afraid, when God is only mentioned, and is concerned lest he go at it tooth and nail. In order that such delusion and timidity may not pursue us he gives us the comforting promise that this king comes meekly.

As if he would say, Do not flee and despair for he does not come now as he came to Adam, to Cain, at the flood, at Babel, to Sodom and Gomorrah, nor as he came to the people of Israel at Mount Sinai; he comes not in wrath, does not wish to reckon with you and demand his debt. All wrath is laid aside, nothing but tenderness and kindness remain. He will now deal with you so that your heart will have pleasure, love, and confidence in him, that henceforth you will much more abide with him and find refuge in him than you feared him and fled from him before. Behold, he is nothing but meekness to you, he is a different man, he acts as if he were sorry ever to have made you afraid and caused you to flee from his punishment and wrath. He desires to reassure and comfort you and bring you to himself by love and kindness.

This means to speak consolingly to a sin-burdened conscience, this means to preach Christ rightly and to proclaim his Gospel. How is it possible that such a form of speech should not make a heart glad and drive away all fear of sin, death, and hell, and establish a free, secure, and good conscience that will henceforth gladly do all and more than is commanded.

29. The evangelist, however, altered the words of the prophet slightly. The prophet says in Zechariah 9:9, "Rejoice greatly, O daughter of Zion; shout, O daughter of Jerusalem: behold, thy king cometh unto thee; he is just, and having salvation; lowly, and riding upon an ass, even upon a colt, the foal of an ass." The evangelist expresses the invitation to joy and exultation briefly in these words, "Tell the daughter of Zion." Further on he leaves out the words, "just and having salvation." Again the prophet says, "he is lowly," the evangelist, "he is meek." The prophet says, "upon the colt, the foal of an ass," he mentions the last word in the plural number; the evangelist says, "upon the colt, the foal of an ass that is used for daily and burden-bearing labor." How shall we harmonize these accounts?

30. First, we must keep in mind that the evangelists do not quote the prophets word by word; it is enough for them to have the same meaning and to show the fulfillment, directing us to the Scriptures so that we ourselves may read, what they omit, and see for ourselves that nothing was written which is not richly fulfilled. It is natural, also, that he who has the substance and the fulfillment, does not care so much for the words. Thus we often find that the evangelists quote the prophets somewhat changed, yet it is done without detriment to the understanding and intent of the original.

31. To invite the daughter of Zion and the daughter of Jerusalem to joy and gladness the prophet abundantly gives us to understand that the coming of this king is most comforting to every sin-burdened conscience, since he

removes all fear and trembling, so that men do not flee from him and look upon him as a severe judge, who will press them with the law, as Moses did, so that they could not have a joyful confidence in God, as the knowledge and realization of sin naturally come from the law. But he would arouse them with this first word to expect from him all grace and goodness. For what other reason should he invite them to rejoice and command them even to shout and be exceeding glad! He tells this command of God to all who are in sorrow and fear of God. He also shows that it is God's will and full intent, and demands that they entertain joyful confidence in him against the natural fear and alarm. And this is the natural voice of the Gospel which the prophet here begins to preach, as Christ speaks likewise in the Gospel and the apostles always admonish to rejoice in Christ, as we shall hear further on.

It is also full of meaning that he comes from the Mount of Olives. We shall notice that this grace on account of its greatness might be called a mountain of grace, a grace that is not only a drop or handful, but grace abundant and heaped up like a mountain.

32. He mentions the people twice while the evangelist says only once, daughter of Zion. For it is one people, daughter of Zion and daughter of Jerusalem, namely, the people of the same city, who believe in Christ and receive him. As I said before, the evangelist quotes the Scriptures only briefly and invites us to read them ourselves and find out more there for ourselves. That the evangelist does not invite to joy like the prophet, but simply says, "Tell it to the daughter of Zion," he does it to show how the joy and exultation shall be carried on. None should expect bodily but spiritual joy, a joy that can be gathered alone from the Word by the faith of the heart. From a worldly aspect there was nothing joyful in Christ's entrance. His spiritual advent must be preached and believed, that is, his meekness; this makes man joyful and glad.

33. That the prophet gives Christ three titles—lowly, just, and having salvation—while the evangelist has only one—meek—is again done for brevity's sake, he suggests more than he explains. It seems to me that the Holy Ghost led the apostles and evangelists to abbreviate passages of the Scriptures for the purpose that we might be kept close to the holy Scriptures, and not set a bad example to future exegetes, who make many words outside the Scriptures and thereby draw us secretly from the Scriptures to human doctrines. As to say, If I spread the Scriptures verbatim everyone will follow the example and it will come to pass that we would read more in other books than in the holy writings of the principal book, and there would be no end to the writing of books and we would be carried from one book to another until, finally, we would get away from the holy Scriptures altogether, as has happened in fact.

Hence with such incomplete quotations he directs us to the original book where they can be found complete, so that there is no need for everyone to make a separate book and leave the first one.

34. We notice, therefore, that it is the intention of all the apostles and evangelists in the New Testament to direct and drive us to the Old Testament, which they call the holy Scriptures proper. For the New Testament was to be only the incarnate living Word and not Scripture. Hence Christ did not write anything himself, but gave the command to preach and extend the Gospel, which lay hidden in the Scriptures, as we shall hear on Epiphany Sunday.

35. In the Hebrew language the two words "meek" and "lowly" do not sound unlike, and mean not a poor man who is wanting in money and property, but who in his heart is humble and wretched, in whom truly no anger nor haughtiness is to be found, but meekness and sympathy. And if we wish to obtain the full meaning of this word, we must take it as Luke uses it, who describes how Christ at his entrance wept and wailed over Jerusalem.

We interpret therefore the words lowly and meek in the light of Christ's conduct. How does he appear? His heart is full of sorrow and compassion toward Jerusalem. There is no anger or revenge, but he weeps out of tenderness at their impending doom. None was so bad that he did or wished him harm. His sympathy makes him so kind and full of pity that he thinks not of anger, of haughtiness, of threatening or revenge, but offers boundless compassion and good will. This is what the prophet calls lowly and the evangelist meek. Blessed he who thus knows Christ in him and believes in him. He cannot be afraid of him, but has a true and comforting confidence in him and entrance to him. He does not try to find fault either, for as he believes, he finds it; these words do not lie nor deceive.

36. The word "just" does not mean here the justice with which God judges, which is called the severe justice of God. For if Christ came to us with this who could stand before him? Who could receive him, since even the saints cannot endure it? The joy and grace of this entrance would thereby be changed into the greatest fear and terror. But that grace is meant, by which he makes us just or righteous. I wish the word *justus, justitia,* were not used for the severe judicial justice; for originally it means godly, godliness. When we say, He is a pious man, the Scriptures express it, He is *justus,* justified or just. But the severe justice of God is called in the Scriptures, severity, judgment, tribunal.

The prophet's meaning, therefore, is this, Thy king cometh to thee pious or just, i.e., he comes to make you godly through himself and his grace; he knows well that you are not godly. Your piety should consist not in your deeds, but in his grace and gift, so that you are just and godly through him. In this sense Saint Paul speaks, in Romans 3:26, "That he might himself be just, and the justifier of him that hath faith in Jesus." That is, Christ alone is pious before God and he alone makes us pious. Also, in Romans 1:17, "For therein is revealed a righteousness of God from faith unto faith," that is the godliness of God, namely, his grace and mercy, by which he makes us godly before him, is preached in the Gospel. You see in this verse from the prophet that Christ is preached for us unto righteousness, that he comes godly and just, and we become godly and just by faith.

37. Note this fact carefully, that when you find in the Scriptures the word God's justice, it is not to be understood of the self-existing, imminent justice of God, as the papists and many of the fathers held, lest you be frightened; but, according to the usage of Holy Writ, it means the revealed grace and mercy of God through Jesus Christ in us by means of which we are considered godly and righteous before him. Hence it is called God's justice or righteousness effected not by us, but by God through grace, just as God's work, God's wisdom, God's strength, God's Word, God's mouth, signifies what he works and speaks in us. All this is demonstrated clearly by Saint Paul, in Romans 1:16, "I am not ashamed of the Gospel of Christ; for it is the power of God (which works in us and strengthens us) unto salvation to everyone that believeth. For therein is revealed a righteousness of God," as it is written in Habakkuk 2:4, "The righteous shall live by his faith." Here you see that he speaks of the righteousness of faith and calls the same the righteousness of God, preached in the Gospel, since the Gospel teaches nothing else but that he who believes has grace and is righteous before God and is saved.

In the same manner you should understand Psalm 31:1, "Deliver me in thy righteousness," i.e., by your grace, which makes me godly and righteous. The word Savior or Redeemer compels us to accept this as the meaning of the little word "just." For if Christ came with his severe justice he would not save anyone, but condemn all, as they are all sinners and unjust. But now he comes to make not only just and righteous, but also blessed, all who receive him, that he alone as the just one and the Savior be offered graciously to all sinners out of unmerited kindness and righteousness.

38. When the evangelist calls his steed a burden-bearing and working foal of an ass he describes the animal the prophets mean. He wants to say, The prophecy is fulfilled in this burden-bearing animal. It was not a special animal trained for this purpose, as according to the country's custom riding animals are trained, and when the prophet speaks of the foal of the ass it is his meaning that it was a colt, but not a colt of a horse.

II. CONCERNING GOOD WORKS

39. We have said enough of faith. We now come to consider good works. We receive Christ not only as a gift by faith, but also as an example of love toward our neighbor, whom we are to serve as Christ serves us. Faith brings and gives Christ to you with all his possessions. Love gives you to your neighbor with all your possessions. These two things constitute a true and complete Christian life; then follow suffering and persecution for such faith and love, and out of these grows hope in patience.

40. You ask, perhaps, What are the good works you are to do to your neighbor? Answer: They have no name. As the good works Christ does to you have no name, so your good works are to have no name.

41. Whereby do you know them? Answer: They have no name, so that there may be no distinction made and they be not divided, that you might do some and leave others undone. You shall give yourself up to him altogether, with all you have, the same as Christ did not simply pray or fast for you. Prayer and fasting are not the works he did for you, but he gave himself up wholly to you, with praying, fasting, all works, and suffering, so that there is nothing in him that is not yours and was not done for you. Thus it is not your good work that you give alms or that you pray, but that you offer yourself to your neighbor and serve him, wherever he needs you and every way you can, be it with alms, prayer, work, fasting, counsel, comfort, instruction, admonition, punishment, apologizing, clothing, food, and, lastly, with suffering and dying for him. Pray, where are now such works to be found in Christendom?

42. I wish to God I had a voice like a thunderbolt, that I might preach to all the world, and tear the word "good works" out of people's hearts, mouths, ears, books, or at least give them the right understanding of it. All the world sings, speaks, writes, and thinks of good works, everyone wishes to exercise themselves in good works, and, yet, good works are done nowhere, no one has the right understanding of good works. Oh, that all such pulpits in all the world were cast into the fire and burned to ashes! How they mislead people with their good works! They call good works what God has not commanded, as pilgrimages, fasting, building and decorating their churches in honor of the saints, saying Mass, paying for vigils, praying with rosaries, much prattling and bawling in churches, turning nun, monk, priest, using special food, raiment or dwelling—who can enumerate all the horrible abominations and deceptions? This is the pope's government and holiness.

43. If you have ears to hear and a mind to observe, pray, listen and learn for God's sake what good works are and mean. A good work is good for the reason that it is useful and benefits and helps the one for whom it is done; why

else should it be called good! For there is a difference between good works and great, long, numerous, beautiful works. When you throw a big stone a great distance it is a great work, but whom does it benefit? If you can jump, run, fence well, it is a fine work, but whom does it benefit? Whom does it help, if you wear a costly coat or build a fine house?

44. And to come to our papists' work, what does it avail if they put silver or gold on the walls, wood, and stone in the churches? Who would be made better if each village had ten bells, as big as those at Erfurt? Whom would it help if all the houses were convents and monasteries as splendid as the temple of Solomon? Who is benefited if you fast for Saint Catherine, Saint Martin, or any other saint? Whom does it benefit if you are shaved half or wholly, if you wear a gray or a black cap? Of what use were it if all people held Mass every hour? What benefit is it if in one church, as at Meissen, they sing day and night without interruption? Who is better for it if every church had more silver, pictures, and jewelry than the churches of Halle and Wittenberg? It is folly and deception; men's lies invented these things and called them good works. They all pretend they serve God thus and pray for the people and their sins, just as if they helped God with their property or as if his saints were in need of our work. Sticks and stones are not as rude and mad as we are. A tree bears fruit, not for itself, but for the good of man and beast, and these fruits are its good works.

45. Hear then how Christ explains good works in Matthew 7:12, "Whatsoever ye would that men should do unto you, even so do ye unto them; for this is the law and the prophets." Do you hear now what are the contents of the whole law and of all the prophets? You are not to do good to God and to his dead saints, they are not in need of it; still less to wood and stone, to which it is of no use, nor is it needed, but to men, to men, to men. Do you not hear? To men you should do everything that you would they should do to you.

46. I would not have you build me a church or tower or cast bells for me. I would not have you construct for me an organ with fourteen stops and ten rows of flute work. Of this I can neither eat nor drink, support neither wife nor child, keep neither house nor land. You may feast my eyes on these and tickle my ears, but what shall I give to my children? Where are the necessaries of life? O madness, madness! The bishops and lords, who should check it, are the first in such folly, and one blind leader leads the other. Such people remind me of young girls playing with dolls and of boys riding on sticks. Indeed, they are nothing but children and players with dolls, and riders of hobbyhorses.

47. Keep in mind that you need not do any work for God nor for the departed saints, but you ask and receive good from him in faith. Christ has done

and accomplished everything for you, atoned for your sins, secured grace and life and salvation. Be content with this, only think how he can become more and more your own and strengthen your faith. Hence direct all the good you can do and your whole life to the end that it be good; but it is good only when it is useful to other people and not to yourself. You need it not, since Christ has done and given for you all that you might seek and desire for yourself, here and hereafter, be it forgiveness of sins, merit of salvation, or whatever it may be called. If you find a work in you by which you benefit God or his saints or yourself and not your neighbor, know that such a work is not good.

48. A man is to live, speak, act, hear, suffer, and die for the good of his wife and child, the wife for the husband, the children for the parents, the servants for their masters, the masters for their servants, the government for its subjects, the subjects for the government, each one for his fellowman, even for his enemies, so that one is the other's hand, mouth, eye, foot, even heart and mind. This is a truly Christian and good work, which can and shall be done at all times, in all places, toward all people. You notice the papists' works in organs, pilgrimages, fasting, etc., are really beautiful, great, numerous, long, wide, and heavy works, but there is no good, useful, and helpful work among them and the proverb may be applied to them, It is already bad.

49. But beware of their acute subtleties, when they say, If these works are not good to our neighbor in his body, they do spiritual good to his soul, since they serve God and propitiate him and secure his grace. Here it is time to say, You lie as wide as your mouth. God is to be worshiped not with works, but by faith; faith must do everything that is to be done between God and us. There may be more faith in a miller-boy than in all the papists, and it may gain more than all priests and monks do with their organs and jugglery, even if they had more organs than these now have pipes. He who has faith can pray for his fellowman, he who has no faith can pray for nothing.

It is a satanic lie to call such outward pomp spiritually good and useful works. A miller's maid, if she believes, does more good, accomplishes more, and I would trust her more, if she takes the sack from the horse, than all the priests and monks, if they kill themselves singing day and night and torment themselves to the quick. You great, coarse fools, would you expect to help the people with your faithless life and distribute spiritual goods, when there is on earth no more miserable, needy, godless people than you are? You should be called, not spiritual, but spiritless.

50. Behold, such good works Christ teaches here by his example. Tell me what does he do to serve himself and to do good to himself? The prophet directs all to the daughter of Zion and says, "He cometh to thee," and that he

comes as a Savior, just and meek, is all for you, to make you just and blessed. None had asked nor bidden him to come; but he came, he comes of his own free will, out of pure love, to do good and to be useful and helpful.

Now his work is manifold, it embraces all that is necessary to make us just and blessed. But justification and salvation imply that he delivers us from sin, death, hell, and does it not only for his friends, but also for his enemies, yea, for none but his enemies, yet he does it so tenderly, that he weeps over those who oppose such work and will not receive him. Hence he leaves nothing undone to blot out their sin, conquer death and hell, and make them just and blessed. He retains nothing for himself, and is content that he already has God and is blessed—thus he serves only us according to the will of his Father, who wishes him to do so.

51. See then how he keeps the law, "Whatsoever ye would that men should do unto you, even so do ye unto them." Is it not true, everyone heartily wishes that another might step between man and his sin, take it upon himself and blot it out, so that it would no more sting his conscience, and deliver him from death and hell? What does everyone desire more deeply than to be free from death and hell? Who would not be free from sin and have a good, joyful conscience before God? Do we not see how all men have striven for this, with prayer, fastings, pilgrimages, donations, monasteries, and priestdom? Who urges them? It is sin, death, hell from which they would be saved. And if there were a physician at the end of the world, who could help here, all lands would become deserted and everyone would hasten to this physician and risk property, body, and life to make the journey.

And if Christ himself, like we, were surrounded by death, sin, and hell, he would wish that someone would help him out of it, take his sin away, and give him a good conscience. Since he would have others do this for him, he proceeds and does it for others, as the law says; he takes upon himself our sins, goes into death, and overcomes for us sin, death, and hell, so that henceforth all who believe in him, and call upon his name, shall be justified and saved, be above sin and death, have a good, joyful, secure, and intrepid conscience forever, as he says in John 8:51, "If a man keep my word, he shall never see death," and John 11:25–26, "I am the resurrection, and the life; he that believeth on me, though he die, yet shall he live, and whosoever liveth and believeth on me, shall never die."

52. Behold, this is the great joy, to which the prophet invites, when he says, "Rejoice greatly, O daughter of Zion; shout, O daughter of Jerusalem!" This is the righteousness and the salvation for which the Savior and king comes. These are the good works done for us by which he fulfills the law. Hence the

death of the believer in Christ is not death but a sleep, for he neither sees nor tastes death, as is said in Psalm 4:8, "In peace will I both lay me down and sleep, for thou, Jehovah, alone makest me dwell in safety." Therefore death is also called a sleep in the Scriptures.

53. But the papists and their disciples, who would get rid of death, sin, and hell by their own works and satisfaction, must remain in them eternally for they undertake to do for themselves what Christ alone did and could do, of whom they should expect it by faith. Therefore they are foolish, deluded people who do works for Christ and his saints, which they should do for their neighbor. Again, what they should expect of Christ by faith they would find in themselves and have gone so far as to spend on stone and wood, on bells, and incense what they should spend on their neighbors. They go on and do good to God and his saints, fast for them, and dedicate to them prayers, and at the same time leave their neighbor as he is, thinking only, let us first help ourselves! Then comes the pope and sells them his letter of indulgence and leads them into heaven, not into God's heaven, but into the pope's heaven, which is the abyss of hell. Behold, this is the fruit of unbelief and ignorance of Christ, this is our reward for having left the Gospel in obscurity and setting up human doctrine in its place. I repeat it, I wish all pulpits in the world lay in ashes, and the monasteries, convents, churches, hermitages and chapels, and everything were ashes and powder because of this shameful misleading of souls.

54. Now you know what good works are. Think of it and act accordingly. As to sin, death, and hell, take care that you augment them not, for you cannot do anything here, your good works will avail nothing, you must have someone else to work for you. To Christ himself such works properly belong; you must consent to it that he who comes is the king of Zion, that he alone is the just Savior. In him and through him you will blot out sin and death through faith. Therefore, if anyone teaches you to blot out your own sin by works, beware of him.

55. When in opposition to this they quote verses of the Bible like Daniel 4:27, "Break off thine iniquities by showing mercy to the poor," and 1 Peter 4:8, "Love covereth a multitude of sins," and the like, be not deceived; such passages do not mean that the works could blot out or remove sin, for this would rob Christ of his word and advent, and do away with his whole work. But these works are a sure work of faith, which in Christ receives remission of sins and the victory over death. For it is impossible for him who believes in Christ, as a just Savior, not to love and to do good. If, however, he does not do good nor love, it is sure that faith is not present. Therefore man knows by

the fruits what kind of a tree it is, and it is proved by love and deed whether Christ is in him and he believes in Christ. As Saint Peter says in 2 Peter 1:10, "Wherefore, brethren, give the more diligence to make your calling and election sure; for if ye do these things, ye shall never stumble," that is, if you bravely practice good works you will be sure and cannot doubt that God has called and chosen you.

56. Thus faith blots out sin in a different manner than love. Faith blots it out of itself, while love or good works prove and demonstrate that faith has done so and is present, as Saint Paul says, in 1 Corinthians 13:2, "And if I have all faith, so as to remove mountains, but have not love, I am nothing." Why? Without doubt, because faith is not present where there is no love, they are not separate the one from the other. See to it then that you do not err and be misled from faith to works.

57. Good works should be done, but we should not confide in them, instead of in Christ's work. We should not touch sin, death, and hell with our works, but direct them from us to the Savior, to the king of Zion, who rides upon an ass. He who knows how to treat sin, death, and hell will blot out sin, overcome death, and subdue hell. Do you permit him to perform these works while you serve your neighbor—you will then have a sure testimony of faith in the Savior who overcame death. So love and good works will blot out your sin for you that you may realize it; as faith blots it out before God where you do not realize it. But more of this later.

The Lesson Story and the False Notions the Jews Held Concerning the Messiah

58. In the story of this Gospel we will first direct our attention to the reason why the evangelist quotes the words of the prophet, in which was described long ago and in clear, beautiful, and wonderful words, the bodily, public entrance and advent of our Lord Jesus Christ to the people of Zion or Jerusalem, as the text says. In this the prophet wanted to show and explain to his people and to all the world, who the Messiah is and how and in what manner he would come and manifest himself, and offers a plain and visible sign in this that he says, "Behold, thy king cometh unto thee, meek, and riding upon an ass," etc., so that we would be certain of it, and not dispute about the promised Messiah or Christ, nor wait for another.

He therewith anticipates the mistaken idea of the Jews, who thought, because there were such glorious things said and written of Christ and his kingdom, he would manifest himself in great worldly pomp and glory, as a king against their enemies, especially the Roman empire, to the power of which they were subject, and would overthrow its power and might, and in their place set up the Jews as lords and princes. They thus expected nothing in the promised Christ but a worldly kingdom and deliverance from bodily captivity. Even today they cling to such dreams and therefore they do not believe in Christ, because they have not seen such bodily relief and worldly power. They were led to this notion, and strengthened in it by their false priests, preachers, and doctors, who perverted the Scriptures concerning Christ and interpreted them according to their own worldly understanding as referring to bodily, worldly things, because they would fain be great earthly lords.

59. But the dear prophets plainly foretold and faithfully gave warning that we should not think of such an earthly kingdom nor of bodily salvation, but look back and pay attention to the promises of a spiritual kingdom and of a redemption from the pernicious fall of mankind in paradise; of which it is said in Genesis 2:17, "In the day that thou eatest thereof thou shalt surely die." The first prophecy of Christ is also against it, in Genesis 3:15, "The seed of woman shall bruise the serpent's head." This means he shall deliver all mankind from the power of the devil and the captivity of sin and eternal death and, instead, bring justification before God and eternal life. Hence this prophet calls him "just and having salvation." This truly is a different salvation from that of bodily freedom, bodily power and glory, the end of which is death, and under which everything must abide eternally.

They ought to have considered this and rejoiced in it, since the prophets had heartily yearned and prayed for it, and this prophet admonishes to such great joy and gladness. But they and their shameless preachers made a temporal affair out of this misery and unhappiness, as if it were a joke about sin and death or the power of the devil, and considered it the greatest misfortune that they lost their temporal freedom and were made subject to the emperor and required to pay taxes to him.

60. The evangelist therefore quotes this saying of the prophet, to punish the blindness and false notions of those who seek bodily and temporal blessings in Christ and his Gospel, and to convince them by the testimony of the prophet, who shows clearly what kind of a king Christ was and what they should seek in him, in that he calls him just and having salvation and yet adds this sign of his coming by which they are to know him, "He cometh to thee meek, and riding upon a colt, the foal of an ass." As if to say, A poor, miserable, almost beggarly horseman upon a borrowed ass who is kept by the side of its mother not for ostentation but for service. With this he desires to lead them away from gazing and waiting for a glorious entrance of a worldly king. And he offers such signs that they might not doubt the Christ, nor take offense at

his beggarly appearance. All pomp and splendor are to be left out of sight, and the heart and the eyes directed to the poor rider, who became poor and miserable and made himself of no kingly reputation that they might not seek the things of this world in him but the eternal, as is indicated by the words, "just and having salvation."

61. This verse first clearly and effectively does away with the Jewish dream and delusion of a worldly reign of the Messiah and of their temporal freedom. It takes away all cause and support for excuse, if they do not receive Christ, and cuts off all hope and expectation for another, because it clearly and distinctly announces and admonishes that he would come on this wise and that he has fulfilled everything. We Christians thus have against the Jews a firm ground and certain title and conviction from their own Scripture that this Messiah, who thus came to them, is the Christ predicted by the prophets and that no other shall come, and that in the vain hope of another's coming they forfeit their temporal and eternal salvation.

III. THE SPIRITUAL INTERPRETATION OF THIS GOSPEL

62. This has been said about the history of this Gospel. Let us now treat of its hidden or spiritual meaning. Here we are to remember that Christ's earthly walk and conversation signify his spiritual walk; his bodily walk therefore signifies the Gospel and the faith. As with his bodily feet he walked from one town to another, so by preaching he came into the world. Hence this lesson shows distinctly what the Gospel is and how it is to be preached, what it does and effects in the world, and its history is a fine, pleasing picture and image of how the kingdom of Christ is carried on by the office of preaching. We will consider this point by point.

And when they drew nigh unto Jerusalem,
and came unto Bethphage, unto the Mount of Olives.

63. All the apostles declare that Christ would become man at the end of the world, and that the Gospel would be the last preaching, as is written in 1 John 2:18, "Little children, it is the last hour, and as ye have heard that Antichrist cometh, even now hath there arisen many Antichrists; whereby we know that it is the last hour," etc. He mentions here the Antichrist. Antichrist in Greek means he who teaches and acts against the true Christ. Again, 1 Corinthians 10:11, "All these things were written for our admonition, upon whom the ends of the ages are come." As the prophets came to man before the first advent of Christ, so the apostles are the last messengers of God, sent before the last advent of Christ at the last day to preach it faithfully. Christ

indicates this by not sending out his apostles to fetch the ass, until he drew nigh unto Jerusalem, where he was now to enter. Thus the Gospel is brought into this world by the apostles shortly before the last day, when Christ will enter with his flock into the eternal Jerusalem.

64. This agrees with the word "Bethphage," which means, as some say, mouth-house, for Saint Paul says in Romans 1:2, that the Gospel was promised afore in the holy Scriptures, but it was not preached orally and publicly until Christ came and sent out his apostles. Therefore the church is a mouth-house, not a pen-house, for since Christ's advent that Gospel is preached orally which before was hidden in written books.

It is the way of the Gospel and of the New Testament that it is to be preached and discussed orally with a living voice. Christ himself wrote nothing, nor did he give command to write, but to preach orally. Thus the apostles were not sent out until Christ came to his mouth-house, that is, until the time had come to preach orally and to bring the Gospel from dead writing and pen-work to the living voice and mouth. From this time, the church is rightly called Bethphage, since she has and hears the living voice of the Gospel.

65. The sending shows that the kingdom of Christ is contained in the public oral office of preaching, which shall not stand still nor remain in one place, as before it was hidden with the Jewish nation alone in the Scriptures and foretold by the prophets for the future, but should go openly, free, and untrammeled into all the world.

66. The Mount of Olives signifies the great mercy and grace of God, that sent forth the apostles and brought the Gospel to us. Olive oil in Holy Writ signifies the grace and mercy of God, by which the soul and the conscience are comforted and healed, as the oil soothes and softens and heals the wounds and defects of the body. And from what was said above, we learn what unspeakable grace it is that we know and have Christ, the justified Savior and king. Therefore he does not send into the level plain, nor upon a deserted, rocky mountain, but unto the Mount of Olives, to show to all the world the mercy which prompted him to such grace. There is not simply a drop or handful of it, as formerly, but because of its great abundance it might be called a mountain. The prophet also calls in Psalm 36:6, such grace God's mountain and says, "Thy righteousness is like the mountains of God," that is, great and abundant, rich and overflowing. This he can understand who considers what it means that Christ bears our sin, and conquers death and hell, and does everything for us that is necessary to our salvation. He does not expect us to do anything for it, but to exercise it toward our neighbor, to know thereby whether we have such faith in Christ or not. Hence the Mount

of Olives signifies that the Gospel was not preached nor sent until the time of grace came; from this time on, the great grace goes out into the world through the apostles.

> *Then Jesus sent two disciples, saying unto them,*
> *"Go into the village that is over against you."*

67. These two disciples represent all the apostles and preachers sent into the world. The evangelical sermon is to consist of two witnesses, as Saint Paul says in Romans 3:21, "A righteousness of God has been manifested, being witnessed by the law and the prophets." Thus we see how the apostles introduce the law and the prophets, who prophesied of Christ, so that it might be fulfilled that Moses spoke in Deuteronomy 17:6 and Christ in Matthew 18:16, "At the mouth of two witnesses or three, every word may be established."

68. When he says, "Go into the village over against you," not mentioning the name, it signifies that the apostles are not sent to one nation alone, as the Jews were separated from the gentiles and alone bore the name "People of God" and God's Word and promise of the future Messiah were with them alone. But now when Christ comes, he sends his preachers into all the world and commands them to go straight forward and preach everywhere to all the heathen, and to teach, reprove, without distinction, whomsoever they meet, however great and wise and learned and holy they may be.

When he calls the great city of Jerusalem a village and does not give her name, he does it for the reason that the name Jerusalem has a holy significance. The kingdom of heaven and salvation are the spiritual Jerusalem that Christ enters. But the apostles were sent into the world among their enemies who have no name.

69. The Lord here comforts and strengthens the apostles and all ministers when he calls the great city a village and adds, she is over against you. As if he would say, like Matthew 10:16, "Behold, I send you forth as sheep in the midst of the wolves," I send you into the world, which is against you, and seems to be something great, for there are kings, princes, the learned, the rich, and everything that is great in the world and amounts to anything, this is against you. And as he says in Matthew 10:22, "Ye shall be hated of all men for my name's sake." But never fear, go on, it is hardly a village, do not be moved by great appearances, preach bravely against it, and fear no one. For it is not possible that he should preach the Gospel truth, who fears the multitude and does not despise all that the world esteems highly. It is here decreed that this village is against the apostles; therefore they should not be surprised if the great, high, rich, wise, and holy orders do not accept their word. It must be

so, the village must be against them; again, the apostles must despise them and appear before them, for the Lord will have no flatterer as a preacher. He does not say, Go around the village, or to the one side of it. Go in bravely and tell them what they do not like to hear.

70. How very few there are now who enter the village that is against them. We gladly go into the towns that are on our side. The Lord might have said: Go ye into the village before you. That would have been a pleasing and customary form of speech. But he would indicate this mystery of the ministry, hence he speaks in an unusual way: Go into the village that is over against you. That is: Preach to them that are disposed to prosecute and kill you. You shall merit such thanks and not try to please them, for such is the way of hypocrites and not that of the evangelists.

"And straightway ye shall find an ass tied, and a colt with her; loose them and bring them unto me."

71. This is also offered as consolation to ministers that they should not worry as to who would believe or receive them. For it is decreed in Isaiah 55:11, "My word shall not return unto me void." And Saint Paul says, in Colossians 1:6, "The Gospel is in all the world bearing fruit." It cannot be otherwise than that where the Gospel is preached there will be some who accept it and believe. This is the meaning of the mystery that the apostles shall find the ass forthwith and the colt, if they only go. As if he would say, Only go and preach, care not who they are that hear you. I will care for that. The world will be against you, but be not afraid, you will find such as will hear and follow you. You do not know them yet, but I know them; you preach, and leave the rest to me.

72. Behold, in this way he consoles them that they should not cease to preach against the world, though it withstands and contradicts them ever so hard, it shall not be in vain. You find people now who believe we should be silent and cause no stir, because it is impossible to convert the world. It is all in vain, they say; pope, priests, bishops, and monks reject it and they will not change their lives; what is the use to preach and storm against them? This is the same as if the apostles had said to Christ, You tell us to go into the village that is over against us; if it is against us, what use is it that we enter there; let us rather stay outside.

But the Lord refutes this and says, Go there and preach, what does it matter if it is against you? You will find there what I say. We should now do likewise. Although the masses storm against the Gospel and there is no hope that they will be better, yet we must preach. There will yet be found those who listen and become converted.

73. Why does he have them bring two asses or not both young or old ones, since one was enough for him to ride upon? Answer: As the two disciples represent the preachers, so the colt and its mother represent their disciples and hearers. The preachers shall be Christ's disciples and be sent by him, that is, they should preach nothing but Christ's doctrine. Nor should they go to preach except they be called, as was the case with the apostles. But the hearers are old and young.

74. Here we should remember that man in Holy Writ is divided into two parts, in an inner and an outer man. The outer man is called according to his outward, visible, bodily life and conversation; the inner man, according to his heart and conscience. The outer man can be forced to do the good and quit the bad, by law, pain, punishment, and shame, or attracted by favor, money, honor, and reward. But the inner man cannot be forced to do out of his own free will, what he should do, except the grace of God change the heart and make it willing.

Hence the Scriptures say all men are liars, no man does good of his own free will, but everyone seeks his own and does nothing out of love for virtue. For if there were no heaven nor hell, no honor nor disgrace, none would do good. If it were as great an honor and prize to commit adultery as to honor matrimony, you would see adultery committed with much greater pleasure than matrimony is now held sacred. In like manner all other sins would be done with greater zeal than virtues are now practiced. Hence all good conduct without grace is mere glitter and semblance; it touches only the exterior man, without the mind and free will of the inner man's being reached.

75. These are the two asses: The old one is the exterior man; he is bound like this one, with laws and fear of death, of hell, of shame, or with allurements of heaven, of life, of honor. He goes forward with the external appearance of good works and is a pious rogue, but he does it unwillingly and with a heavy heart and a heavy conscience.

Therefore the apostle calls her *"subjugalem,"* the yoked animal, who works under a burden and labors hard. It is a miserable, pitiable life that is under compulsion by fear of hell, of death, and of shame. Hell, death, and shame are his yoke and burden, heavy beyond measure, from which he has a burdened conscience and is secretly an enemy to law and to God. Such people were the Jews, who waited for Christ, and such are all who rely upon their own power to fulfill God's commands, and merit heaven. They are tied by their consciences to the law; they must, but would rather not, do it. They are carriers of sacks, lazy beasts of burden, and yoked rogues.

76. The colt, the young ass, of which Mark and Luke write, on which never man rode, is the inner man, the heart, the mind, the will, which can never be subject to law, even if he be tied by conscience and feels the law. But he has no desire nor love for it until Christ comes and rides on him. As this colt was never ridden by anyone, so man's heart has never been subject to the good; but, as Moses says in Genesis 6:5 and 8:21, is evil continually from his youth.

77. Christ tells them to loose them, that is, he tells them to preach the Gospel in his name, in which is proclaimed grace and remission of sins, and how he fulfilled the law for us. The heart is here freed from the fetters of conscience and things. Thus man is loose not from the law, that he should and joyful, willing, and anxious to do and to leave undone all things. Thus man is loose not from the law, that he should do nothing, but from a joyless, heavy conscience he has from the law, and with which he was the enemy of the law, that threatens him with death and hell. Now he has a clear conscience under Christ, is a friend of the law, neither fears death nor hell, does freely and willingly, what before he did reluctantly. See, in this way the Gospel delivers the heart from all evil, from sin and death, from hell, and a bad conscience through faith in Christ.

78. When he commands them to bring them to him, he speaks against the pope and all sects and deceivers, who lead the souls from Christ to themselves; but the apostles bring them to Christ; they preach and teach nothing but Christ, and not their own doctrine nor human laws. The Gospel alone teaches us to come to Christ and to know Christ rightly. In this the stupid prelates receive a heavy rebuke at their system of bringing souls to themselves, as Paul says, in Acts 20:29–30, "I know that after my departing grievous wolves shall enter in among you, not sparing the flock; and from among your own selves shall men arise, speaking perverse things, to draw away the disciples after them." But the Gospel converts men to Christ and to none else. Therefore he sends out the Gospel and ordains preachers, that he may draw us all to himself, that we may know him as he says, in John 12:32, "And I, if I be lifted up from the earth, will draw all men unto myself."

> *"And if any man say aught unto you, ye shall say,*
> *The Lord hath need of them; and straightway he will send them."*

79. Saint Paul, in Galatians 4:2, compares the law to guardians and stewards, under whom the young heir is educated in fear and discipline. The law forces with threats that we externally abstain from evil works, from fear of death and hell, although the heart does not become good thereby. Here are, as

Luke writes, the masters of the ass and its colt, speaking to the apostles, What, do ye loose the colt? Where the Gospel begins to loose the conscience of its own works, it seems to forbid good works and the keeping of the law. It is the common speech of all the teachers of the law, and of the scribes and doctors, to say, If all our works amount to nothing and if the works done under the law are evil, we will never do good. You forbid good works and throw away God's law; you heretic, you loose the colt and wish to make bad people free. Then they go to work and forbid to loose the colt and the conscience and to bring it to Christ and say, You must do good works, and keep people tied in bondage to the law.

80. Our text shows how the apostles should act toward such persons. They should say, "The Lord hath need of them." They should instruct them in the works of the law and the works of grace, and should say, We forbid not good works, but we loose the conscience from false good works, not to make them free to do evil deeds, but to come under Christ, their true Master and, under him, do truly good works; to this end he needs them and will have them. Of this Paul treats so well in Romans 6, where he teaches that through grace we are free from the law and its works; not so as to do evil, but to do truly good works.

81. It all amounts to this, that the scribes and masters of the law do not know what good works are; they therefore will not loose the colt, but drive it with unmerciful human works. However, where wholesome instruction is given concerning good works, they let it pass, if they are at all sensible and honest teachers of the law, as they are here represented. The mad tyrants, who are frantic with human laws, are not mentioned in this Gospel. It treats only of the law of God and of the very best teachers of the law. For without grace, even God's law is a chain and makes burdened consciences and hypocrites whom none can help, until other works are taught, which are not ours, but Christ's, and are worked in us by grace. Then all constraint and coercion of the law is ended and the colt is loose.

Now this is come to pass, that it might be fulfilled, which was spoken through the prophet, saying, "Tell ye the daughter of Zion."

82. This verse has already been sufficiently explained. The evangelist introduces it that we may see how Christ has come not for the sake of our merits, but for the sake of God's truth. For he was prophesied long ago before we, to whom he comes, had a being. God out of pure grace has fulfilled the promises of the Gospel to demonstrate the truth that he keeps his promises in order to stir us confidently to trust in his promise, for he will fulfill it.

And this is one of the passages, where the Gospel is promised, of which Paul speaks in Romans 1:2, "Which he promised afore through his prophets in the holy Scriptures, concerning his Son Jesus Christ," etc. We have heard how in this verse the Gospel, Christ, and faith are preached most distinctly and consolingly.

And the disciples went, and did even as Jesus appointed
them, and brought the ass, and the colt, and put on them their
garments, and he sat thereon, (and they set him thereon).

83. These are the ministers who by the Gospel have freed the consciences from the law and its works and led them to the works of grace, who made real saints out of hypocrites, so that Christ henceforth rides upon them.

84. The question arises here, whether Christ rode upon both animals. Matthew speaks as if the disciples put him on both, while Mark, Luke, and John mention only the colt. Some think he sat first on the colt and, because it was too wanton and untamed, he then sat on its mother. These are fables and dreams. We take it that he rode only on the colt. He had them both brought to him on account of the spiritual significance above mentioned. When Matthew says he sat on them as though he rode on both, it is said after the manner of the Scriptures and the common way of speaking by synecdoche, where a thing is ascribed to the community, the whole people, which applies only to a few of them; for example, Matthew writes, The thieves on the cross reviled him, while only one did it, as Luke tells us. Christ says in Matthew 23:37 that the city of Jerusalem stoned the prophets, while only a few of the city did it. You say, the Turks [Muslims] killed the Christians, although they killed only a few. Thus Christ rode on the asses, though he rode only on the colt, because the two are compared to a community. What happened to one is expressed as if it happened to all.

85. Now consider the spiritual riding. Christ rides on the colt, its mother follows, that is, when Christ lives through faith in the inner man we are under him and are ruled by him. But the outer man, the ass, goes free, Christ does not ride on her, though she follows in the rear. The outer man, as Paul says, is not willing; he strives against the inner man; nor does he carry Christ, as Galatians 5:17 says, "The flesh lusteth against the Spirit, and the Spirit against the flesh; for these are contrary, the one to the other; that ye may not do the things that ye would." Because the colt carries Christ, that is, the Spirit is willing by grace, the ass, that is, the flesh, must be led by the halter, for the Spirit chastises and crucifies the flesh, so that it becomes subject.

86. This is the reason Christ rides upon the colt and not upon its mother, and yet uses both for his entrance into Jerusalem, for both body and soul must

be saved. If, here upon earth, the body is unwilling, not capable of grace and Christ's leading, it must bear the Spirit, upon which Christ rides, who trains it and leads it along by the power of grace, received through Christ. The colt, ridden by Christ, upon which no one ever rode, is the willing spirit, whom no one before could make willing, tame, or ready, save Christ by his grace. However, the sack-carrier, the burden-bearer, the old Adam, is the flesh, which goes riderless without Christ; it must for this reason bear the cross and remain a beast of burden.

87. What does it signify that the apostles, without command, put their garments on the colt? No doubt again not all the disciples laid on their garments, nor were all their garments put on, perhaps only a coat of one disciple. But it is written for the spiritual meaning, as if all the garments of all the disciples were used. It was a poor saddle and ornaments, but rich in meaning. I think it was the good example of the apostles, by which the Christian Church is covered, and adorned, and Christ is praised and honored, namely, their preaching and confession, suffering and death for Christ's sake, as Christ says of Peter, that he would glorify God by a like death, in John 21:19. Paul says in one of his Epistles, we shall put on Christ, by which he doubtless wishes to show that good works are the garments of the Christians, by which Christ is honored and glorified before all people. In the Epistle, Paul says, in Romans 13:12, "Let us put on the armor of light." By this he means to show that good works are garments in which we walk before the people, honorably and well adorned. The examples of the apostles are the best and noblest above all the saints; they instruct us best and teach Christ most clearly. Therefore they should not, like the rest, lie on the road, but on the colt, so that Christ may ride on them and the colt go under them. We should follow these examples, praise Christ with our confession and our life, and adorn and honor the doctrine of the Gospel as Titus 2:10 says.

88. Hear how Paul lays his garments on the colt in 1 Corinthians 11:1, "Be ye imitators of me, even as I also am of Christ," and in Hebrews 13:7, "Remember them that had the rule over you, men that spake unto you the Word of God; and considering the issue of their life, imitate their faith." No saint's example is as pure in faith as that of the apostles. All the other saints after the apostles have an addition of human doctrine and works. Hence Christ sits upon their garments to show that they are true Christian and more faithful examples than others.

89. That they set him thereon must also signify something. Could he not mount for himself? Why does he act so formal? As I said above, the apostles would not preach themselves, nor ride on the colt themselves. Paul says, in 2

Corinthians 1:24, "Not that we have lordship over your faith." And in 2 Corinthians 4:5, "We preach not ourselves, but Christ Jesus as Lord, and ourselves as your servants for Jesus' sake." Again, in 1 Peter 5:3, "Neither as lording it over the charge allotted to you." They preached to us the pure faith and offered their examples, that Christ might rule in us, and our faith remain undefiled, that we might not receive their word and work as if it were their own, but that we might learn Christ in their words and works. But how is it today? One follows Saint Francis, another Saint Dominic, the third this, and the fourth that saint; and in none is Christ alone and pure faith sought; for they belong only to the apostles.

And the most part of the multitude spread their garments in the way;
and others cut branches from the trees, and spread them in the way.

90. The garments are the examples of the patriarchs and prophets, and the histories of the Old Testament. For, as we shall learn, the multitude that went before, signifies the saints before the birth of Christ, by whom the sermon in the New Testament and the way of faith are beautifully adorned and honored. Paul does likewise when he cites Abraham, Isaac, Jacob, and Peter cites Sarah and, in Hebrews 11, many patriarchs are named as examples, and by these are confirmed faith and the works of faith in a masterly way. The branches mean the sayings of the prophets, one of which is mentioned in this Gospel, which are not stories nor examples but the prophecy of God. The trees are the books of the prophets. Those who preach from these cut down branches and spread them in the way of Christian faith.

91. All this teaches the character of an evangelical sermon, a sermon on the pure faith and the way of life. It must first have the word Christ commands the apostles, saying, Go, loose and bring hither. Then the story and example of the apostles must be added that agree with Christ's word and work—these are the garments of the apostles. Then must be cited passages from the Old Testament—these are the garments and branches of the multitude. In this way the passages and examples of both Testaments are brought home to the people. Of this Christ speaks in Matthew 13:52, "Every scribe who hath been made a disciple to the kingdom of heaven, is like unto a man that is a householder, who bringeth forth out of his treasure things new and old." This signifies the two lips of the mouth, the two points of a bishop's hat, the two ribbons on it, and some other like figures. But now none of these is kept before the eyes, the devil through the papists throws sulphur and pitch in the way, himself rides on the colt and banishes Christ.

92. To spread garments in the way means that, following the example of the apostles, we should with our confession and our whole life, honor,

adorn, and grace Christ by giving up all glory, wisdom, and holiness of our own and bowing to Christ in simple faith; also that we turn everything we have— honor, goods, life, power, and body—to the glory and advancement of the Gospel, and relinquish everything for the one thing needful. Kings and lords and the great, powerful, and rich should serve Christ with their goods, honor, and power; further the Gospel and for its sake abandon everything. The holy patriarchs, prophets, and pious kings in the Old Testament did so by their examples. But now everything is turned around, especially among the papal multitudes, who usurp all honor and power against Christ and thus suppress the Gospel.

93. To cut branches from the trees and spread them in the way means also the office of preaching and the testimony of the Scriptures and the prophets concerning Christ. With this the sermon of Christ is to be confirmed and all the preaching directed to the end that Christ may be known and confessed by it. John writes in John 12:13, that they took branches of palm trees and went forth to meet him. Some add, there must have been olive branches also, because it happened on the Mount of Olives. This is not incredible, although the Gospels do not report it.

94. There is reason why palm branches and olive branches are mentioned. They signify what is to be confessed, preached, and believed concerning Christ. It is the nature of the palm tree that when used as a beam, it yields to no weight but rises against the weight. These branches are the words of divine wisdom; the more they are suppressed, the higher they rise. This is true if you firmly believe in those words. There is an invincible power in them, so that they may well be called palm branches, as Saint Paul says in Romans 1:16, "The Gospel is the power of God unto salvation to everyone that believeth," and, as Christ says, "The gates of hell shall not prevail against it," in Matthew 16:18. Death, sin, hell, and all evil must bend before the divine Word, or only rise, when it sets itself against them.

95. Olive branches are named, because they are words of grace in which God has promised us mercy. They make the soul meek, gentle, joyful, as the oil does the body. The gracious Word and sweet Gospel is typified in Genesis 8:11, where the dove in the evening brought in her mouth an olive branch with green leaves into the ark, which means the Holy Spirit brings the Gospel into the church at the end of the world by the mouth of the apostles.

And the multitudes that went before him, and that followed,
cried, saying, "Hosanna to the son of David: Blessed is he that
cometh in the name of the Lord; Hosanna in the highest."

96. For this reason they carried palm trees before kings and lords, when they had gained a victory and celebrated their triumph. Again, the carrying of palm branches was a sign of submission, especially of such as asked for mercy and peace, as was commonly done among ancient people.

By their pomp before Christ they indicated that they would receive him as their Lord and king, sent by God as a victorious and invincible Savior, showing themselves submissive to him and seeking grace from him. Christ should be preached and made known in all the world, as the victorious and invincible king against sin, death, and the power of the devil and all the world for those who are oppressed and tormented, and as a Lord with whom they shall find abundant grace and mercy, as their faithful priest and mediator before God.

The word of the Gospel concerning this king is a word of mercy and grace, which brings us peace and redemption from God, besides invincible power and strength, as Saint Paul in Romans 1:16, calls the Gospel "a power of God unto salvation" and "the gates of hell shall not prevail against it," as Christ says in Matthew 16:18.

97. Paul says, in Hebrews 13:8, "Jesus Christ is the same yesterday and today, yea, forever." All who will be saved from the beginning to the end of the world, are and must be Christians and must be saved by faith. Therefore Paul says, in 1 Corinthians 10:3–4, "Our fathers did all eat the same spiritual food; and did all drink the same spiritual drink." And Christ says in John 8:56, "Your father Abraham rejoiced to see my day; and he saw it and was glad."

98. Hence the multitudes going before signify all Christians and saints before Christ's birth; those who follow signify all the saints after the birth of Christ. They all believed in and adhered to the one Christ. The former expected him in the future, the latter received him as the one who had come. Hence they all sing the same song and praise and thank God in Christ. Nor may we give anything else but praise and thanks to God, since we receive all from him, be it grace, word, work, Gospel, faith, and everything else. The only true Christian service is to praise and give thanks, as Psalm 50:15 says, "Call upon me in the day of trouble, I will deliver thee, and thou shalt glorify me."

99. What does "Hosanna to the son of David" signify? Hosanna in Psalm 118:25–26, means, "Save now, we beseech thee, O Jehovah; O Jehovah, we beseech thee, send now prosperity. Blessed be he that cometh in the name of Jehovah." This verse was applied to Christ and is a well-wishing as we wish happiness and safety to a new ruler. Thus the people thought Christ should be their worldly king, and they wish him joy and happiness to that end. For "hosanna" means, O, give prosperity or Beloved, help or Beloved, save or whatever else you might desire to express in such a wish. They add, "to the

son of David," and say, God give prosperity to the son of David! O God, give prosperity, blessed be, etc. We would say, O, dear Lord, give happiness and prosperity to this son of David, for his new kingdom! Let him enter in God's name that he may be blessed and his kingdom prosper.

100. Mark proves clearly that they meant his kingdom when he writes expressly in Mark 11:10 that they said, "Blessed is the kingdom that cometh, the kingdom of our father David: Hosanna in the highest." When some in the churches read it "Osanna," it is not correct; it should be "Hosanna." They made a woman's name out of it, and her whom they should call Susanna they call Osanna. Susanna is a woman's name and means a rose. Finally, after making a farce out of baptism, the bishops baptize bells and altars, which is a great nonsense, and call the bells Osanna. But away with the blind leaders! We should learn here also to sing Hosanna and Hazelihana to the son of David together with those multitudes, that is, joyfully wish happiness and prosperity to the kingdom of Christ, to holy Christendom, that God may put away all human doctrine and let Christ alone be our king, who governs by his Gospel, and permits us to be his colts! God grant it, Amen.

The Second Sunday in Advent

⚜

The Comfort Christians Have from the Signs of the Day of Judgment; and the Spiritual Interpretation of These Signs

And there shall be signs in the sun and moon and stars; and upon the earth distress of nations, in perplexity for the roaring of the sea and the billows; men fainting for fear, and for expectation of the things which are coming on the world: for the powers of the heavens shall be shaken. And then shall they see the Son of man coming in a cloud with power and great glory. But when these things begin to come to pass, look up, and lift up your heads; because your redemption draweth nigh."

And he spake to them a parable: "Behold the fig tree, and all the trees: when they now shoot forth, ye see it and know of your own selves that the summer is now nigh. Even so ye also, when ye see these things coming to pass, know ye that the kingdom of God is nigh. Verily I say unto you, This generation shall not pass away, till all things be accomplished. Heaven and earth shall pass away: but my words shall not pass away." — LUKE 21:25–36

I. THE SIGNS OF THE DAY OF JUDGMENT

1. The first thing for us to understand is that although the signs preceding the judgment day are many and great, they will all be fulfilled, even though none or very few men take note of or esteem them as such. For two things must take place according to the Word and prophecy of Christ and the apostles: first, that many and great signs will be made manifest; and secondly, that the last day will come unawares, the world's not expecting it, even though that day be at the door. Though men see these signs, yea, be told that they are signs of the last day, still they will not believe, but in their security mockingly say, "Thou fool, hast thou fear that the heavens will fall and that we shall live to see that day?"

2. Some, indeed, must see it, and it will be those who least expect it. That there will be such security and indifference among men, let us prove by the words of Christ and the apostles. Christ says in the 34th and 35th verses of Luke 21, "Take heed to yourselves, lest haply your hearts be overcharged with surfeiting, and drunkenness, and cares of this life, and that day come on you suddenly as a snare: for so shall it come upon all them that dwell on the face of all the earth." From these words it is clear that men in great measure will give themselves over to surfeiting and drunkenness and the cares of this life, and that, drowned as it were in these things, they will rest secure and continue to dwell on the earth as if the dreadful day were far away. For, were there no such security and heedlessness, that day would not break in unawares. But he says, it will come as a snare by which birds and beasts are caught at a time when most concerned about their food and least expecting to be entrapped. In this figure he gives us clearly to understand that the world will continue its carousing, eating and drinking, building and planting, and diligently seeking after earthly things, and will look upon the day of judgment as yet a thousand and more years off, when, in the twinkling of an eye, they may stand before the terrible judgment bar of God.

3. The words of Christ in Luke 17:24, say the same: "For as the lightning, when it lighteneth out of the one part under the heaven, shineth unto the other part under heaven; so shall the Son of man be in his day." See here again that the day will break upon the world with the utmost suddenness. The same further appears in what follows in verses 26–29: "As it was in the days of Noah, even so shall it be also in the days of the Son of man. They ate, they drank, they married, they were given in marriage, until the day that Noah entered into the ark, and the flood came, and destroyed them all. Likewise even as it came to pass in the days of Lot; they ate, they drank, they bought, they sold, they planted, they builded; but in the day that Lot went out from Sodom it rained fire and brimstone from heaven, and destroyed them all. After the same manner it shall be in the day that the Son of man is revealed." These words abundantly show that people will rest so secure and will be so deeply buried beneath the cares of this life, that they will not believe the day is at hand.

4. There is now no doubt that Christ did not foretell these signs in the expectation that no one would note nor recognize them when they should appear; although few indeed will do so, just as in the days of Noah and Lot but few knew the punishment in store for them. Were this not true, the admonition of Christ would have been in vain: "When ye see these things come to pass, know ye that the kingdom of God is nigh." Then, "Lift up your heads, because your redemption draweth nigh." There must then be some,

at least, who do recognize the signs, and lift up their heads and wait for their redemption, although they do not really know on what day that will come. We should be careful, therefore, to note whether the signs are being fulfilled now, or have been or will be in the future.

5. I do not wish to force anyone to believe as I do; neither will I permit anyone to deny me the right to believe that the last day is near at hand. These words and signs of Christ compel me to believe that such is the case. For the history of the centuries that have passed since the birth of Christ nowhere reveals conditions like those of the present. There has never been such building and planting in the world.

There has never been such gluttonous and varied eating and drinking as now. Wearing apparel has reached its limit in costliness. Who has ever heard of such commerce as now encircles the earth? There have arisen all kinds of art and sculpture, embroidery and engraving, the like of which has not been seen during the whole Christian era.

6. In addition men are so delving into the mysteries of things that today a boy of twenty knows more than twenty doctors formerly knew. There is such a knowledge of languages and all manner of wisdom that it must be confessed, the world has reached such great heights in the things that pertain to the body, or as Christ calls them, "cares of life"—eating, drinking, building, planting, buying, selling, marrying, and giving in marriage—that everyone must see and say either ruin or a change must come. It is hard to see how a change can come. Day after day dawns and the same conditions remain. There was never such keenness, understanding, and judgment among Christians in bodily and temporal things as now—I forbear to speak of the new inventions, printing, firearms, and other implements of war.

7. But not only have such great strides been made in the world of commerce, but also in the spiritual field have there been great changes. Error, sin, and falsehood have never held sway in the world as in these last centuries. The Gospel has been openly condemned at Constance, and the false teachings of the pope have been adopted as law though he practiced the greatest extortion. Daily Mass is celebrated many hundred thousand times in the world, and thereby the greatest sin committed. By confession, sacrament, indulgence, rules, and laws, so many souls are driven to condemnation that it seems God has given the whole world over to the devil. In short, it is not possible that there should be greater falsehood, more heinous error, more dreadful blindness, and more obdurate blasphemy than have ruled in the church through the bishops, cloisters, and universities. As a result, Aristotle, a blind heathen, teaches and rules Christians more than does Christ.

8. Moreover the pope has attempted to abolish Christ and to become his vicar. He occupies the throne of Christ on earth, would to God he occupied the devil's throne instead.

I forbear to speak of the grosser forms of sin, unchastity, murder, infidelity, covetousness, and the like, which are all practiced without shame or fear. Unchastity has taken forms against nature, and has affected no station or condition more than the spiritual character of the clergy—shall I call it spiritual, since it is so fleshly and void of all simplicity?

9. Whatever other signs may appear before Christ's coming, I know that, according to the words of Christ, these will be present: surfeiting and drunkenness, building and planting, buying and selling, marrying and giving in marriage, and other cares of this life. Just as certain to me is also the saying of Christ in Matthew 2:15, where he speaks of the abomination of desolation, the Antichrist, under whose rule gross error, blindness, and sin shall flourish, just as they now flourish under the pope in the most tyrannical and shameless form. This above all else compels me to believe that Christ will soon come to judgment; for such sins cry to heaven, and so provoke and defy the last day that it must soon break in upon them.

If it were only the unchastity of the antediluvian world, or the worldliness of Sodom, I would not believe the last day is so near at hand. But to destroy, root out, condemn, and blaspheme divine service, God's Word and the sacraments, the children of God, and everything that belongs to God; and to worship and honor the devil instead and to proclaim his lies for the Word of God—such sins, I am firmly convinced, will put an end to the world before we are aware of it. Amen.

10. But the apostles have also prophesied concerning this self-security of men as the judgment day approaches. Paul says in 1 Thessalonians 5:2–3, "The day of the Lord so cometh as a thief in the night. When they are saying, Peace and safety, then sudden destruction cometh upon them." Now we know that a thief never comes but when one feels most secure and least expects him. And, in 2 Peter 3:3–10, we read, "In the last days mockers shall come with mockery, walking after their own lusts, and saying, Where is the promise of his coming? From the day the fathers fell asleep, all things continue as they were from the beginning of the creation. . . . But the day of the Lord will come as a thief in the night; in the which the heavens shall pass away with a great noise, etc." Who are they that walk after their own lusts but the papal clergy? They wish to be subject neither to God nor to man, but expect the world to recognize it as their right to live as they please and to do what they like. It is these that say, Where is the promise of his coming? Do

you think the last day will break in upon us so soon? Things will continue as they have in the past.

11. We also read in the history of the destruction of Jerusalem that many signs were fulfilled, yet they would not believe them to be tokens of the coming destruction until judgment was executed. Finally, from the beginning of the world, it has ever been so, that the unbelieving could not believe the day of calamity to be near—they always experienced it before they believed it. This is in fulfillment of Psalm 55:23, "Bloodthirsty and deceitful men shall not live out half their days," for they presume upon the continuance of their days and have no fear, and so the hour must come unawares. So here people are putting off the judgment for yet a thousand years when it may break in upon them in a night. This is the first class of signs that presage the nearness of the day of God. Let us now consider the second class.

"And there shall be signs in the sun."

12. This sign to be given in the sun is that it will lose its brightness, after the manner in which it has often occurred, as Matthew 24:29 says, "The sun shall be darkened." I will not trespass here again but express my opinion. Some think that the sun is to be darkened as never to shine again; but this cannot be the meaning, for day and night must continue to the end, as God foretells, in Genesis 8:22, "While the earth remaineth, seedtime and harvest, and cold and heat, and summer and winter, and day and night shall not cease." This sign must, therefore, not interfere with day and night and still be fulfilled before the judgment day, for it is a token of its coming. It cannot, therefore, be more than a darkening of the sun in its accustomed course.

13. Now at all times such a sign in the sun has been looked upon as foreboding misfortune or disaster, which also often followed, as history abundantly shows. Thus we have had, it seems to me, the last few years more and more frequent eclipses of the sun than in any other like period of time. God has spared us and no great evil has come upon us. For this reason these signs are not noticed. In addition, astronomers have told us, and rightly so, that these eclipses are but natural phenomena. As a result the tokens are still more despised and carnal security increased. Nevertheless God, in carrying on his work in silence, gives us security and moves forward in his plans. Whatever the natural course of the heavens may be, these signs are always tokens of his wrath and predict sure disaster for the future. If these are not seen, shall God make other suns and moons and stars and show other signs in them?

14. The course of the heavens has been so arranged from eternity that be-fore the last day these signs must appear. The heathen say that the comet is

a natural product; but God has created none that is not a token of future evil.
Thus also the blind leader, Aristotle, writing a book about the phenomena
of the heavens, attributes all to nature and declares these are no signs. Our
learned men follow him and thus one fool fills the world with fools. Let us
know that though the heavenly bodies wander in their courses according to
law, God has still made these to be signs or tokens of his wrath.

"And in the moon."

15. This sign is given in Matthew 24:29, to the effect that "the moon shall
not give her light"; that is, it will lose its brightness. The same is to be said of
this as of the signs in the sun, no matter how natural it may be. Is it not true
that scarcely a year has passed of late in which sun or moon or both have been
eclipsed, sometimes one of them twice a year? If these are not signs, then,
what are signs? It may be that at other times more were seen than now, but
surely not in more rapid succession. When Jerusalem was to be destroyed,
some signs preceded that had occurred before, but they were still new tokens.

"And in the stars."

16. According to Matthew 24:29, "the stars shall fall from heaven." This is
seen almost daily. Whether it was seen as frequently in former days as now, I
cannot say. Aristotle again talks about the nature of the thing; but the Gospel,
which is the Word and wisdom of God, pronounces the falling of the stars a
sign and there let the matter rest. Wherefore if the stars fall or the sun and
moon fail to give their light, be assured that these are signs of the last day;
for the Gospel cannot utter falsehood. While in these years there have been
so many showers of stars, they are all harbingers of the last day, just as Christ
says; for they must appear often in order that the great day may be abundantly
pointed out and proclaimed. These signs appear and pass but no one considers them; so it shall be that they will wait for other signs just as the Jews are
waiting for another Christ.

"And upon the earth distress of nations, in perplexity."

17. This is not to be understood that all nations and all people among
these nations will so suffer; for you must note that these are to be signs. Stars
do not fall from the heavens at all times; the sun does not lose its brightness
for a whole year or a month, but for an hour or two; the moon does not refuse
to give its light for a whole week or a whole night, but, like the sun, for an
hour or two—that all these may be tokens without changing or perverting
the order of things. Hence not many will suffer distress and anxiety, but only

a few; and even with these it will be only at times that they be signs to those who despise the idea, and attribute all to the complexion or to the melancholy or to the influence of the planets or to any other natural cause. Meanwhile such clear harbingers of the day pass by unobserved, and there happens what Christ said of the Jews in Matthew 13:14, that though hearing and seeing they do not understand.

18. "Distress of nations in perplexity" does not refer to the body. For, as we have already heard, there will be peace and joy in abundance. People will eat and drink, build and plant, buy and sell, marry and be given in marriage, dance and play, and wrap themselves up in this present life as if they expected to abide here forever. I take it that it is the condition of agonized conscience. For since the Gospel, by which alone the troubled conscience can be comforted, is condemned, and in its stead there are set up doctrines of men, which teach us to lay aside sin and earn heaven by works, there must come a burdened and distressed conscience, a conscience that can find no rest, that would be pious, do good and be saved, that torments itself and yet does not know how to find satisfaction. Sin and conscience oppress, and however much is done no rest is found. By these the sinner becomes so distressed that he knows not what to do nor whither to flee. Hence arise so many vows and pilgrimages and worship of the saints and chapters for Mass and vigils. Some castigate and torture themselves, some become monks, or that they may do more they become Carthusian monks.

These are all works of distressed and perplexed consciences, and are in reality the distress and perplexity of which Luke here speaks. He uses two words which suggest this meaning, a man gets into close quarters as though he were cast into a narrow snare or prison; he becomes anxious and does not know how he may extricate himself; he becomes bewildered and attempts this and that and yet finds no way of escape. Under such conditions he would be distressed and perplexed. In such a condition are these consciences; sin has taken them captive, they are in straits and are distressed. They want to escape but another grief overtakes them, they are perplexed for they know not where to begin—they try every expedient but find no help.

19. It is indeed true that the masses do not become so afflicted, but only the few and generally the most sensible, scrupulous, and good-hearted individuals who have no desire to harm anyone and would live honorable lives. It may be they foster some secret sin, as for example unchastity. This burdens them day and night so that they never are truly happy. But this is game for the monks and priests, for here they can practice extortion, especially with women; here people confess, are taught, absolved, and go whithersoever the

confessor directs. Meanwhile the people are the Lord's token of the last day. To such the Gospel is light and comfort while it condemns the others.

20. Neither can anyone deny this sign, for it has been so common these hundreds of years that many have become insane over it, as Gerson informs us. Although at all times there have been people so distressed and perplexed, it was formerly not so common as now. From the beginning of the world no human doctrine exercised the tenth part or even the hundredth part of the influence, or tortured and seared so many consciences as the doctrines of the pope and his disciples, the monks and priests. Such perplexed hearts will necessarily grow out of the papal doctrine of confession, which has never been so earnestly promulgated as now. Therefore this has never been a token of the judgment until now. There must be many and great signs, therefore, and they be despised by most men.

"For the roaring of the sea and the billows."

21. This will take place through the winds, for all roaring of the waters comes by means of the storm. Therefore the Lord would say by these words that many and great storms will arise. By sea, however, is not to be understood simply the ocean but all gathered waters, according to the language of Scripture, in Genesis 1:10, "And the gathering together of the waters called he seas," be they oceans, seas, or lakes. Rivers, on the other hand, are changeable flowing waters.

22. It is not to be supposed that all waters, streams, lakes, seas, and oceans, will, at the same time and in the same way, become stormy and boisterous. Some seas are thus to be moved and this is to be the sign unto us. For as not all stars fall and not all nations are distressed in perplexity, so shall not all waters roar nor all places be visited by the storm.

23. Here heathen art will sit in the schools and with wide-open mouth will say, "Did you see the storm or hear the sea and the waves roaring? Aristotle clearly teaches that these are but natural phenomena." Let us pass these by and know that God's Word and tokens are despised by the wisdom of the gods. Do you hold fast to the Gospel—this teaches you to believe that storms and detonations in the sea are signs and tokens. And however many times such signals have been given in other days, they shall nevertheless become more numerous and terrible as the day of doom approaches.

24. It seems to me that within the space of ten or twelve years, there have been such storms and tempests and waters roaring as have never before been seen or heard. We are to consider, therefore, that although in former times these signs came singly and at less frequent intervals, now they appear many

and frequent. In our time both sun and moon are darkened, stars fall, distress of nations is present, winds and waves are roaring, and many other signs are being fulfilled. They are all coming in a heap.

25. We have lately also seen so many comets and so many calamities have fallen from the skies and there has arisen the hitherto unknown disease, syphilis. Also how many signs and wonders have been seen in the heavens, as suns, moons, stars, rainbows, and many other strange sights. Dear hearer, let them be signs, great signs, tokens that mean much; so that neither the astronomers nor heathen astrologers can say they simply follow the ordinary course of nature, for they knew nothing of them before nor did they prophesy of them.

26. No astronomer will say that the course of the heavens foretold the coming of the terrible beast that the Tiber threw up a few years ago; a beast with the head of an ass, the breast and body of a woman, the foot of an elephant for its right hand, with the scales of a fish on its legs, and the head of a dragon in its hinder parts, etc. This beast typifies the papacy and the great wrath and punishment of God. Such a mass of signs presages greater results than the mind of man can conceive.

Before proceeding further it might be well to consider the testimony concerning the last day which the celebrated teacher, Latantius Firmianus, gave about AD 320, in his work entitled *"Divinarum Institutionum,"* in the seventh book and fifteenth chapter: When the end of the world draws near, the condition of human affairs must materially change and take on a more wicked form. Then will malice and wickedness prevail to such a degree that our age, in which malice and wickedness have almost reached their highest pitch, will be looked upon as happy and treasured as golden in comparison with that time when no one will be able to help or give advice. Then will righteousness become practically unknown, and blasphemy, covetousness, impure desires, and unchastity become common. Then will the godly become a prey to the most wicked and be vexed and grieved by them. At the same time only the wicked will be rich and well to do, while the godly will be driven hither and thither in shame and poverty. Justice will be perverted, law will be overthrown, and no one will have aught else but that which he can secure by his own strength. Daring and strength will possess all. There will be neither faith nor confidence left in man, neither peace, nor loveliness, nor shame, nor truth, and as a result, no safety, no government, no rest of any kind from the reprobate. For all lands will become rebellious, everywhere men will rage and war with one another, the whole world will be in arms, and bring destruction to itself.

*"Men fainting for fear, and for expectation of the things
which are coming on the world."*

27. Here, again, it is not the profligate mass who disregard God's tokens and refer all to natural causes that shall realize these, but rather the better class, and the most distinguished, who take these things to heart and are given to reflection. By "men fainting for fear" is to be understood that they shall be frightened to death, or the next thing to death; and that their fear shall consume them and rob them of their strength. What do they fear and wait for? Christ says, "The things which are coming on the world"; that is, the last day, the terrible judgment, hellfire, and eternal death. Why do they fear and look for these things, and not the world upon whom they will come rather than upon them? Because these are the tokens of God that are to be despised and rejected by the world.

28. I am not yet able to say who these people are, unless it be those who are exposed to and have to do with the temptations of death and hell, concerning whom Tauler writes. For such temptations consume flesh and blood, yea, bone and marrow, and are death itself. No one can endure them except he be miraculously sustained. A number of patriarchs have tasted them—Abraham, Isaac, Jacob, Moses, David; but near the end of the world they will be more common. This token will then greatly increase, although it is present now more than is generally known. There are individuals who are in the perils of death and are wrestling with him; they feel that which will come over the whole world and fear that it will come upon and abide with them. It is to be hoped, however, that such people are in a state of grace. For Christ speaks as if he would separate the fear and the thing which they fear; and so divides these that he gives to them the fear and to the world that which they fear. It is to be presumed that by this fear and anxiety, they are to have their hell and death here, while the world, which fears nothing, will have death and hell hereafter.

"For the powers of the heavens shall be shaken."

29. By the powers of heaven some understand the angels of heaven. But since Christ speaks of signs, and says we shall see them and in them recognize the coming of the last day, they must surely be visible tokens and be perceived with the bodily senses. For those people whose consciences are in distress and whose hearts are failing from fear, though this be an affection of the soul, yet manifest it by word and countenance. Therefore these powers of heaven must be such as can be really shaken and so perceived.

30. But the Scriptures speak in a twofold way concerning the powers of heaven. At one time they are spoken of as the powerful heavens or the heavens which are among all creatures the most powerful, as is written, in Genesis 1:8,

"And God called the firmament"—that is, expanse or fortress—"heaven"; for every creature under heaven is ruled and strengthened by the light, heat, and movements of the heavens. What would the earth be without the heavens but a dark and desert waste? Like princes and nobles in the world, the Scriptures call the heavens powerful because they rule over the bodies beneath them.

31. At another time, the powers of heaven signify the hosts of heaven, as Psalm 33:6 says, "By the word of Jehovah were the heavens made, and all the host of them by the breath of his mouth." And in Genesis 2:1, "And the heavens and the earth were finished, and all the host of them." It is the common custom of the Scriptures to speak in this way of the powers of heaven. And it is clear from these passages that the hosts or powers of heaven include all that is in them; in the heavens, the sun, moon, stars, and other heavenly bodies; on earth, man and beast, birds and fish, trees, herbs, and whatever else lives upon it.

32. The passage before us may therefore mean the powers of heaven in both senses, probably chiefly the hosts of heaven. Christ would say that all creatures shall be shaken and shall serve as tokens of that day; sun and moon with darkening, the stars with falling, the nations with wars, men with hearts failing from fear, the earth with earthquakes, the waters with winds and roaring, the air with infection and pestilence, and the heavens with their hosts.

33. I do not know just what is meant by the moving of the hosts of heaven unless it be manifestations like those of the great constellation of the planets in 1524. For the planets are certainly among the most important of the powers and hosts of heaven, and their remarkable gathering together into one constellation is surely a token for the world. Christ does not say that all the hosts of heaven will be moved, but some of them only; for not all stars shall fall from their places, nor all men be overcome with fear, nor all waters at the same time be in noisy commotion, nor sun and moon be every day darkened; for these are to be but signs, which can occur only at particular times and in a few places, that they may be something special, and singled out as tokens from the great mass that are not such. It is quite probable, therefore, that these movements of the powers of heaven are such movements of the constellations of the planets. Astrologers interpret them to signify the coming of another flood; God grant that they may rather presage the coming of the last day.

34. Let us not be mistaken, however, and think that these constellations are the product of the natural course of the heavenly bodies. As such Christ calls them signs and desires us to take special note of them, appearing, as they do, not alone but with a multitude of other tokens. Let the unbeliever doubt and despise God's tokens and speak of them as simply natural; but let us hold fast to the Gospel.

35. There are many other signs elsewhere described in the Scriptures, such as earthquakes, famine, pestilence, and wars as in Luke 17:20 and Matthew 24:7. We have seen much of these for they have been common at all times. Still they are tokens appearing by the side of others. It is a known fact also that wars at the present time are of such a character as to make former wars appear as mere child's play. But since our Gospel of today does not speak of these, let us not consider them further. Only let us consider them as signs, great signs, signifying great things; alas, they are already despised and forgotten!

"And then shall they see the Son of man
coming in a cloud with power and great glory."

36. Here power may again signify the hosts of angels, saints, and all creatures that will come with Christ to judgment (I believe this is the correct interpretation); or it may mean the special power and might that will characterize this coming of Christ in contradistinction to his first coming. He says not only that he will come, but that they shall see him come. At his birth he came also, but men did not recognize him. He comes now through the Gospel in a spiritual manner, into the hearts of believers. This also is not by observation. But his last coming will be such that all must see him as Revelation 1:7 says, "And every eye shall see him." And they shall see that he is none other than the man Christ Jesus, in bodily form, as he was born of the Virgin Mary and walked upon this earth.

He might have said they shall see me, but that would not have clearly indicated his bodily form. But when he says, "They shall see the Son of man," he clearly indicates that it will be a bodily coming, a bodily seeing in bodily form; a coming in great power and glory, accompanied by the hosts of heaven. He shall sit upon the clouds and be accompanied by all the saints. The Scriptures speak much of that day and everywhere point to the same. This, then, is said concerning the signs. The Savior adds words of comfort for Christians in the presence of these signs.

II. THE COMFORT CHRISTIANS HAVE WHEN THESE SIGNS APPEAR

"And when these things begin to come to pass, look up,
and lift up your heads; because your redemption draweth nigh."

37. Here you may say, who can lift up his head in the face of such terrible wrath and judgment? If the whole world is filled with fear at that day, and lets

fall its head and countenance out of terror and anxiety, how shall we look up and lift up our heads, which evidently means, how shall we manifest any joy in and longing for these signs? In answer I would say that all this is spoken only to those who are really Christians and not to heathen and Jews. True Christians are so afflicted with all manner of temptations and persecutions that in this life they are miserable. Therefore they wait and long and pray for redemption from sin and all evil; as we also pray in the Lord's Prayer, "Thy kingdom come," and "Deliver us from evil." If we are true Christians, we will earnestly and heartily join in this prayer. If we do not so pray, we are not yet true Christians.

38. If we pray aright, our condition must truly be such that, however terrible these signs may be, we will look up to them with joy and earnest desire, as Christ admonishes, "When these things begin to come to pass, look up." He does not say, Be filled with fear or drop your heads; for there is coming that for which we have been so earnestly praying. If we really wish to be freed from sin and death and hell, we must look forward to this coming of the Lord with joy and pleasure.

Saint Paul also says, in 2 Timothy 4:8, "Henceforth there is laid up for me the crown of righteousness, which the Lord, the righteous judge, shall give to me at that day: and not only to me, but also to all them that have loved his appearing." If he gives the crown to those who love his appearing, what will he give to those who hate and dread it? Without doubt, to enemies, eternal condemnation. Titus 2:13 says, "Looking for the blessed hope and appearing of the glory of the Great God and our Savior Jesus Christ." And in Luke 12:6, "And be ye yourselves like unto men looking for their lord, when he shall return from the marriage feast."

39. But what do those do who are filled with fear and do not desire to have him come, when they pray, "Thy kingdom come, thy will be done," and "Deliver us from the evil one"? Do they not stand in the presence of God and lie to their own hurt? Do they not strive against the will of God who will have this day for the redemption of the saints? It is necessary, therefore, that we exercise great care lest we be found to hate and to dread that day. Such dread is a bad omen and belongs to the damned, whose cold minds and hard hearts must be terrified and broken, if perchance they might reform.

40. But to believers that day will be comforting and sweet. That day will be the highest joy and safety to the believer, and the deepest terror and anguish to the unbeliever; just as also in this life the truths of the Gospel are exceedingly sweet to the godly and exceedingly hateful to the wicked. Why should the believer fear and not rather exceedingly rejoice, since he trusts in Christ who comes as judge to redeem him and to be his everlasting portion.

41. But you say I would indeed await his coming with joy, if I were holy and without sin. I should answer, what relief do you find in fear and flight? It would not redeem you from sin if you were to be filled with terror for a thousand years. The damned are eternally filled with fear of that day, but this does not take away their sin; yea, this fear rather increases sin and renders man unfit to appear without sin on that day when it comes. Fear must pass out of the soul and there must enter in a desire for righteousness and for that day. But if you really desire to be free from sin and to be holy, then give thanks to God and continue to desire to be more free from sin. Would to God that such desire were so sincere and powerful in you as to bring you to your death.

42. There is no one so well prepared for the judgment day as he who longs to be without sin. If you have such desire, what do you fear? You are then in perfect accord with the purpose of that day. It comes to set free from sin all who desire it, and you belong to that number. Return thanks to God and abide in that desire. Christ says his coming is for our redemption. But do not deceive yourself and be satisfied, perhaps, with the simple desire to be free from sin and to await the coming of the day without fear. Perhaps your heart is false and you are filled with fear, not because you would be free from sin, but because in the face of that day you cannot sin free and untrammeled. See to it that the light within you be not darkness. For a heart that would be truly free from sin will certainly rejoice in the day that fulfills its desire. If the heart does not so rejoice there is no true desire to be loosed from its sin.

43. Therefore we must above all things lay aside all hatred and abhorrence of this day, and exercise diligence that we may really desire to have our sins taken away. When this is done, we may not only calmly await the day, but with heartfelt desire and joy pray for it and say, "Thy kingdom come, thy will be done." In this you must cast aside all feelings and conceit, hold fast to the comforting words of Christ, and rest in them alone.

44. Could he admonish, comfort, and strengthen you in a more delicate and loving manner? In the first place he says, You will hear of wars, but you should have no fears. And when he tells you to have no fears, what else does he mean than that he commands you to be of good cheer and to discern the signs with joy? Secondly, he tells you to look up; thirdly, to lift up your heads; and fourthly, he speaks of your redemption. What can comfort and strengthen you if such a word does not? Do you think he would deceive you and try to lead you into a false confidence? My dear hearer, let such a word not have been said in vain: thank God and trust in it—there is no other comfort or advice if you cast this to the winds. It is not your condemnation but your redemption of which Christ speaks. Will you turn his words around and say,

It is not your redemption but your condemnation? Will you flee from your own salvation? Will you not greet and thank your God who comes out to meet and to greet you?

45. He has no doubt also spoken this word for the fainthearted who, although they are devout and prepared for the last day, are yet filled with great anxiety and are hindered in taking part in his coming with that desire that should be found at the end of the world; therefore he calls attention to their redemption. For when at the end of the world sin will hold such sway, and by the side of sin the punishment for sin with pestilence, war, and famine, it will be necessary to give to believers strength and comfort against both evils, sin and its punishment. Therefore he uses the sweet and comforting word redemption which is so dear to the heart of man. What is redemption? Who would not be redeemed? Who would have a desire to abide in the desert of sin and punishment? Who would not wish an end to such misery and woe, such perils for souls, such ruin for man? Especially should this be the case when the Savior allures, invites, and comforts us in such an endearing way.

46. The godless fanatical preachers are to be censured who in their sermons deprive people of these words of Christ and faith in them, who desire to make people devout by terrifying them and who teach them to prepare for the last day by relying upon their good works as satisfaction for their sins. Here despair, fear, and terror must remain and grow and with it hatred, aversion, and abhorrence for the coming of the Lord, and enmity against God be established in the heart; for they picture Christ as nothing but a stern judge whose wrath must be appeased by works, and they never present him as the Redeemer, as he calls and offers himself, of whom we are to expect that out of pure grace he will redeem us from sin and evil.

47. Such is always the result where the Gospel is not rightly proclaimed. When hearts are only driven by commands and threats, they will only be estranged from God and be led to abhor him. We ought to terrify, but only the obstinate and hardened; and when these have become terrified and dejected also, we ought to strengthen and comfort.

48. From all this we learn how few there are who pray the Lord's Prayer acceptably even though it is prayed unceasingly in all the world. There are few who would not rather that the day would never come. This is nothing else than to desire that the kingdom of God may not come. Therefore the heart prays contrary to the lips, and while God judges according to the heart, they judge according to the lips. For this reason they institute so many prayers, fill all the churches with their bawling, and think they pray aright when in reality their prayer is, "May thy kingdom not come, or not just yet." Tell me, is not

such a prayer blasphemy? Is it not of such a prayer that the psalmist speaks in Psalm 109:7, "Let his prayer be turned into sin." How men are applying all the wealth of the world to fill every nook and corner of it with such blasphemy, and then are calling it a divine service!

49. Yet he who feels such fear must not despair, but rather use it wisely. He uses it wisely who permits such fear to urge and admonish him to pray for grace that this fear might be taken away and he be given joy and delight in that day. Christ has promised, in Matthew 7:8, "Everyone that asketh receiveth." Therefore those who are fearful are nearer their salvation than the hard-hearted and reprobate, who neither fear nor find comfort in that day. For though they do not have a desire for it, they have a something within which admonishes them to pray for such a desire.

50. On the other hand, he uses fear unwisely who allows it to increase and abides in the same, as though he could thereby be cleansed from sin. This leads to nothing good. Not fear, which, as John says, in 1 John 4:18, must be cast out, will remain in that day, but love which, Saint Paul says in 1 Corinthians 13:8, must abide. Fear is to be a power to drive us to seek such love and pray for it. Where fear is not cast out, it opposes the will of God and antagonizes your own salvation; it thus becomes a sin against the Holy Spirit. It is, however, not necessary to say that the individual must be altogether without fear, for we still have human nature abiding in us. This is weak and cannot exist altogether without the fear of death and the judgment; but the spirit must be uppermost in the mind, as Christ says, in Matthew 26:41, "The spirit indeed is willing, but the flesh is weak."

> And he spake to them a parable: "Behold the fig tree, and all the trees: when they now shoot forth, ye see it and know of your own selves that the summer is now nigh. Even so ye also, when ye see these things coming to pass, know ye that the kingdom of God is nigh."

51. Pure words of comfort are these. He does not put forth a parable from the fall or winter season when all the trees are bare and the dreary days begin; but a parable from the spring and summer season, when everything is joyous, when all creation buds forth and rejoices. By this he clearly teaches that we are to look forward to the last day with as much joy and delight as all creation shows in spring and summer. What is the meaning of this parable if in it he does not teach us this? He could have found others that were not so joyous.

52. In applying it, he does not say your hell or condemnation is at hand, but the kingdom of God. What else does it signify that the kingdom of God is at hand than that our redemption is near? The kingdom of God is but

ourselves, as Christ says, in Luke 17:21, "For lo, the kingdom of God is within you"; therefore, it draws nigh when we are nearing our redemption from sin and evil. In this life it begins in the spirit; but since we must still battle with sin and suffer much evil, and since death is still before us, the kingdom of God is not yet perfect in us. But when once sin and death and all evil are taken away, then will it be perfect. This the last day will bring and not this life.

53. Therefore, my dear hearer, examine your life, probe your heart to ascertain how it is disposed toward this day. Do not put your trust in your own good life, for that would soon be put to shame; but think of and strengthen your faith so that the day may not be a terror to you as to the damned, but be your joy as the day of your salvation and of the kingdom of God in you. Then when you think or hear of the same, your heart will leap for joy and earnestly long for its coming. If you do not wish to pronounce judgment upon yourself, then do not think that you would be able to stand in that day even with the meritorious deeds of all the saints.

"Verily I say unto you, This generation shall not pass
away, till all things be accomplished. Heaven and earth shall
pass away: but my words shall not pass away."

54. Why does the Lord so fortify his Word and confirm it beyond measure by parables, oaths, and tokens of the generation that shall remain though heaven and earth pass away? This all happens because, as was said above, all the world is so secure and with open eyes despises the signs to such a degree that perhaps no word of God has been so despised as this that foretells and characterizes the judgment day. It will appear to the world that there are no signs; and even though people should see them, they will still not believe. Even the very elect of God may doubt such words and tokens, in order that the day may come when the world is never so secure and thus be suddenly overwhelmed in its security, as Saint Paul said above.

55. Therefore, Christ would assure us and wake us up to look for the day when the signs appear. We are to realize that though the signs be uncertain, those are not in danger who look upon them as tokens, while those who despise them are in the greatest danger. Hence let us play with certainties and consider the above-named signs as truly such lest we run with the unspiritual. If we are mistaken, we have after all hit the mark; if they are mistaken, it is a mistake for eternity with them.

56. Jesus calls the Jews "this generation." This passage, therefore, clearly indicates that the common saying is not true which holds that all the Jews will become Christians; and that the passage, John 10:16, "And they shall become

one flock and one shepherd," is not fulfilled when the Jews go over to the heathen, but when the heathen came to the Jews and became Christians at the time of the apostles, as Saint Augustine often explains. Christ's words in John 10:16, indicate the same, "And other sheep I have, which are not of this fold; them also I must bring, and they shall hear my voice, and they shall become one flock and one shepherd." Note that he speaks clearly of the heathen who have come to the Jewish fold; therefore, the passage has been long since fulfilled. But here he says, "This generation shall not pass away" until the end come; that is, the Jews who crucified Christ must remain as a token. And although many will be converted, the generation and Jewish character must remain.

57. Some have also been concerned about how heaven and earth will pass away, and they again call Aristotle to their aid. He must interpret the words of Christ for them, and he says that heaven and earth will not pass away as to their essence but only as to their form. How much they think they are saying! If they so understood it that heaven and earth will continue to be something, they would indeed be right. But let us suffer the blind to go, and know that just as our bodies will be changed as to their essence, and yet be remade according to their essence, so heaven and earth at the last day with all the elements will be melted with fervent heat and turned to dust, together with the bodies of men, so that there will be nothing but fire everywhere. Then will everything be new-created in greatest beauty; our bodies will shine in brilliancy, and the sun be much more glorious than now. Peter speaks of this day, in 2 Peter 3:10–13, "But the day of the Lord will come as a thief; in the which the heavens shall pass away with a great noise, and the elements shall be dissolved with fervent heat, and the earth and the works that are therein shall be burned up. But, according to his promise, we look for new heavens and a new earth, wherein dwelleth righteousness."

Paul also testifies to the same in 1 Corinthians 3:13, that "the last day shall be revealed in fire." And in Isaiah 30:26, "The light of the moon shall be as the light of the sun, and the light of the sun shall be sevenfold as the light of seven days, in the day that Jehovah bindeth up the hurt of his people, and healeth the stroke of their wound." Likewise in Isaiah 65:17, "For, behold I create new heavens and a new earth; and the former things shall not be remembered, nor come into mind. But be ye glad and rejoice forever in that which I create." Therefore, this passing away is not only according to form but also as to essence; unless it be that you do not want to call it a passing away, if things turn to dust until no trace of them can be found, as the burned body turns to ashes and passes away.

58. But where do our souls dwell when the abode of every creature is afire and there is no earthly dwelling place? Answer: My dear hearer, where is the soul now? Or where is it when we sleep and are not conscious of what is taking place in our bodies and in the world around us? Do you think that God cannot so preserve or hold the souls of men in his hand that they will never know how heaven and earth passed away? Or do you think that he must have a bodily home for the soul, just as a shepherd has a stable for his sheep? It is enough for you to know that they are in God's hands and not in the care of any creature. Though you do not understand how it happens, do not be led astray. Since you have not yet learned what happens to you when you fall asleep or awaken, and can never know how near you are to waking or sleeping, though you daily do both, how do you expect to understand all about this question? The Scripture says, "Father, into thy hands I commend my spirit," and so let it be. Meanwhile there will arise a new heaven and a new earth, and our bodies will be revived again to eternal salvation. Amen. If we knew just how the soul would be kept, faith would be at an end. But now we journey and know not just whither; yet we put our confidence in God, and rest in his keeping, and our faith abides in all its dignity.

III. THE SPIRITUAL INTERPRETATION OF THESE GOSPEL SIGNS

59. Finally, we must find also a hidden or spiritual meaning in this Gospel. The sun is Christ, the moon is the church, the stars are Christians, the powers of heaven are the prelates or planets of the church. Now these earthly signs surely signify what has long since taken place and is now taking place among Christians; for they follow the service of sin and threaten and manifest the punishment resting upon them.

60. That the sun is darkened no doubt signifies that Christ does not shine in the Christian Church; that is, that the Gospel is not preached and that faith is expiring from the lack of divine service. This has come about through the teaching and works of men. The pope sits in the churches in the place of Christ and shines like dirt in a lantern—he with his bishops, priests, and monks. It is these that have darkened the sun for us, and instead of the true worship of God have set up idolatry and image worship with their tonsure and hoods and vestments and pipes and lutes and singing and playing, etc. Oh, what darkness! What darkness!

61. From this, it necessarily follows that neither the moon gives any light; that is, when faith died out, love had to die out, also, so that no real Christian deeds are any more seen, no example is found in which one Christian serves

another; but all the people have been led into idolatry, and image worship, and there have been instituted Mass, vigils, altars, chapels, purifications, bells, and impostures. Again, what darkness!

62. I interpret the falling of the stars to mean the falling of man who has been baptized and become a Christian and then became a priest or monk. Whoever wants to believe me, may; whoever does not want to, need not do so, but I know what I am talking about. I do not say that they will all be lost; God can save even from the fire whom he will. But this I say, whoever becomes a priest or monk in the belief that he is taking up a holy estate falls from Christian faith into unbelief; for the falling of the stars does not signify the gross forms of sin, murder, adultery, theft, but a falling from faith. Priests and monks (unless God does wonders) are by virtue of their position renegade and apostate Christians, worse than whom no people dwell on the earth.

63. The Turks [Muslims] also are no Christians; but in two senses they are better than the papists: first, they have never been Christians or stars, therefore have not fallen from the faith; secondly, they do not sin against the sacrament of the Lord's body and blood. But the papists make a sacrifice out of the Mass and a meritorious work and do it daily and continually. This is certainly the most sacrilegious perversion upon which the sun has yet shined. In short, he who desires to become holy and be saved by works and holy orders, falls from the faith, falls from heaven; for the blood of Jesus Christ alone is able to save us. Therefore, whenever you see a star fall, then know that it signifies someone has become a priest, a monk, or a nun.

64. That men's hearts failed them for fear signifies the torments that the pope's saints and fallen stars suffer, for while they do great things their consciences are never at rest. The Scriptures say they are weary and heavy laden.

65. The roaring winds and seas are the worldly estates, both high and low. There is no ruler or land at peace with the other, no faith or trust in one another, everyone is looking only to his own interests. Neither is there reproof or discipline or fear upon the earth; and the whole world is so engaged in eating, drinking, unchastity, and the lusts of the flesh that it moans and roars.

66. The powers of heaven are our planets, our spiritual squires and tyrants, popes, bishops, and their companions, the universities, which are all so deeply sunk in worldly affairs, property, honor, and pleasures, that they think they are not planets, that is, errorists, for *planeta* in Greek means an errorist, one who does not travel on the right way, but travels backward and to both sides as the planets also do in the heavens. This the Germans express in a proverb—the more learned, the more perverse; in other words, the spiritual government is only planets. But now when the Gospel shines forth and shows

them their virtue and colors it with its own hue, and shows that they are unlearned idolaters and soul-deceivers, they get angry, begin to move, and form a constellation. They gather together, try to shelter themselves behind bulls and edicts, and threateningly predict a great flood. But it will do them no good; the day will come and its light cannot be placed under a bushel like a candle.

67. The parable of the fig tree seems to me to signify that the fig tree is the holy Scriptures that have so long been hidden in obscurity. They are now budding forth and taking leaves, their word is breaking forth into fruitage. For twelve centuries it has not been so well known, nor have its languages been so well known. There is no doubt in my mind, however, that the Scriptures are a fig tree that is easily preserved. It was fig leaves with which Adam and Eve covered their nakedness; for the old Adam always uses the Scriptures to adorn himself. Therefore the book must come forth, its leaves must become green, in spite of all the movements of the planets. The summer is not far distant—would to God that the fruit would also follow the leaves. I fear that there will be nothing but leaves, for we talk much about true faith but bring forth no fruit.

68. Enough has now been said concerning these signs; if anyone desires to consider the matter further, to him has been given here the impulse and a start. But the planets with their factious spirit will not believe in them, in order that the Scriptures may still be true in this, that they give these people great security and contempt for the Word, works, and signs of God.

The Third Sunday in Advent

❦

Christ's Answer to the Question John Asked Him, His Praise of John, and the Application of This Gospel

N ow when John heard in the prison the works of the Christ, he
sent by his disciples and said unto him, "Art thou he that cometh,
or look we for another?" And Jesus answered and said unto them, "Go
and tell John the things which ye hear and see: the blind receive their
sight, and the lame walk, the lepers are cleansed and the deaf hear, and
the dead are raised up, and the poor have good tidings preached to them.
And blessed is he, whosoever shall find no occasion of stumbling in me."

And as these went their way, Jesus began to say unto the multitudes
concerning John, "What went ye out into the wilderness to behold?
a reed shaken with the wind? But what went ye out to see? a man
clothed in soft raiment? Behold, they that wear soft raiment are in
kings' houses. But wherefore went ye out? to see a prophet? Yea, I say
unto you, and much more than a prophet. This is he, of whom it is
written, Behold, I send my messenger before thy face, who shall prepare
thy way before thee." — MATTHEW 11:2–10

I. THE QUESTION JOHN PUTS TO CHRIST

1. The most I find on this Gospel treats of whether John the Baptist knew
that Jesus was the true Christ, although this question is unnecessary and of
little import. Saint Ambrose thinks John asked this question neither in ignorance nor in doubt, but in a Christian spirit. Jerome and Gregory write that
John asked whether he should be Christ's forerunner also into hell, an opinion
that has not the least foundation, for the text plainly says, "Art thou he that
cometh or look we for another?" This looking or waiting for Christ, according
to the words, relates to his coming on earth and pertains to the Jewish people,
otherwise John ought to have asked, or do those in hell look for thee? And
since Christ with his works answered that he had come, it is certain that John
inquired about Christ's bodily coming, as Christ himself thus understood it

and answered accordingly, although I do not deny that Christ also descended into hell, as we confess in our creed.

2. Hence it is evident John knew very well that Jesus was he that should come, for he had baptized him and testified that Christ was the Lamb of God that takes away the sin of the world, and he had also seen the Holy Spirit descending upon him as a dove, and heard the voice from heaven, "This is my beloved Son, in whom I am well pleased." All is fully related by all four evangelists. Why, then, did John ask this question? Answer: It was not done without good reasons. In the first place, it is certain that John asked it for the sake of his disciples, as they did not yet hold Christ to be the one he really was. And John did not come in order to make disciples and draw the people to himself, but to prepare the way for Christ, to lead everybody to Christ, and to make all the people subject to him.

3. Now the disciples of John had heard from him many excellent testimonies concerning Christ, namely, that he was the Lamb of God and the Son of God, and that Christ must increase while he must decrease. All this his disciples and the people did not yet believe, nor could they understand it, as they themselves and all the people thought more of John than of Christ. For this reason they clung so strongly to John, even to the extent that they for his sake became jealous and dissatisfied with Christ when they saw that he also baptized, made disciples, and drew the people to himself. They complained to John about this because they feared that their master would grow less in esteem, as we read, in John 3:26, "And they came unto John and said to him, Rabbi, he that was with thee beyond the Jordan, to whom thou hast borne witness, behold, the same baptizeth, and all men come to him."

4. To this error they were led by two reasons—first, because Christ was not yet known to the people, but only to John; neither had he as yet performed any miracle, and no one was held in high esteem but John. Hence it appeared so strange to them that he should point them and everybody else away from himself and to someone else, inasmuch as there was no one living besides John who had gained a great name and enjoyed great fame. The other reason was because Christ appeared so very humble and common, being the son of a poor carpenter and of a poor widow. Neither did he belong to the priesthood, nor to the learned, but was only a layman and a common apprentice. He had never studied, was brought up as a carpenter apprentice just like other laymen; hence it seemed as though the excellent testimony of John concerning Christ and the common layman and apprentice, Jesus of Nazareth, did not at all harmonize with each other. Therefore, though they believed that John told the truth, they still reasoned, Perhaps it will be someone else than this Jesus,

and they looked for one who might appear among them in an imposing way, like a highly learned leader among the priests, or a mighty king. From such delusion John could not deliver them with his words. They clung to him, and regarded Christ as being much inferior, meanwhile looking for the glorious appearing of the great person of whom John spoke. And should he really be Jesus, then he had to assume a different attitude; he must saddle a steed, put on bright spurs, and dash forward like a lord and king of Israel, just as the kings aforetime had done. Until he should do this, they would cling to John.

5. But when Jesus began to perform miracles and became famous, then John thought he would point his disciples away from himself and lead them to Christ, so they might not think of establishing a new sect and becoming Johnites; but that all might cling to Christ and become Christians, John sends them to Christ so that from now on they might learn not only from the witness he bore of Christ but also from the words and deeds of Christ himself that he was the one of whom John had spoken. It should not be expected that the works and coming of Christ would be attended by drums and bugles and like worldly pomp, but by spiritual power and grace, so there would be no riding and walking on streets paved and carpeted; but by virtue of such power and grace the dead would be raised up, the blind receive their sight, the deaf hear, and all kinds of bodily and spiritual evil be removed. That should be the glory and coming of this king, the least of whose works could not be performed by all the kings, all the learned, and all the rich in the world. This is the meaning of the text.

*Now when John heard in the prison the works of the Christ,
he sent by his disciples and said unto him, "art thou he that cometh,
or look we for another?"*

6. As though John would say to his disciples, There you hear of his works, such as I never accomplished, nor anyone else before him. Now go to him and ask him whether he is the one that cometh. Put away the gross worldly deception that he would ride on steeds in armor. He is increasing, but I must now decrease; my work must cease, but his must continue. You must leave me and cling to him.

7. How necessary it was for John to point his disciples away from himself to Christ is very clear. For what benefit would it have been to them if they had depended a thousand times on John's piety and had not embraced Christ? Without Christ there is no help or remedy, no matter how pious men may be. So at the present day what benefit is it to the monks and nuns to observe the rules of Saint Benedict, Saint Bernard, Saint Francis, Saint Dominic, and Saint Augustine if they do not embrace Christ and him only, and depart also

from their John? All Benedictines, Carthusians, Barefoot-Friars, Ecclesiastes, Augustinians, Carmelites, all monks and nuns are surely lost, as only Christians are saved. Whoever is not a Christian even John the Baptist cannot help, who, indeed, according to Christ, was the greatest of all saints.

8. However, John deals kindly with his disciples and has patience with their weak faith until they shall have grown strong. He does not condemn them because they do not firmly believe him. Thus we should deal with the consciences of men ensnared by the examples and regulations of pious men until they are freed from them.

II. CHRIST'S ANSWER, GIVEN IN WORDS AND DEEDS

And Jesus answered and said unto them, "Go and tell John the things which you hear and see; the blind receive their sight, and the lame walk, the lepers are cleansed, and the deaf hear, and the dead are raised up, and the poor have good tidings preached to them. And blessed is he whosoever shall find no occasion of stumbling in me."

9. Christ answered John also for the sake of his disciples. He answers in a twofold way: first, by his works; secondly, by his words. He did the same thing when the Jews surrounded him in the temple and asked him, "If thou art the Christ, tell us plainly," in John 10:24. But he points them to his works, saying, "I told you, and ye believe not, the works that I do in my Father's name, these bear witness of me," in John 10:25. Again, "Though ye believe not me, believe the works," in John 10:38. Here Christ first points them to the works, and then also to the words, saying, "And blessed is he, whosoever shall find no occasion of stumbling in me." With these words, he does not only confess that he is the Christ, but also warns them against finding occasion of stumbling in him. If he were not the Christ, then he who finds no occasion of stumbling in him could not be blessed. For one can dispense with all the saints, but Christ is the only one that no man can dispense with. No saint can help us, none but Christ.

10. The answer of his works is more convincing, first, because such works were never before accomplished either by John or by anyone else; and secondly, because these works were predicted by the prophets. Therefore, when they saw that it came to pass just as the prophets had foretold, they could and should have been assured. For thus Isaiah had said of these works, "The Spirit of the Lord Jehovah is upon me, because Jehovah hath anointed me to preach good tidings unto the weak; he hath sent me to bind up the broken-hearted, to proclaim liberty to the captives, and the opening of the prison to them that are bound," in Isaiah 61:1. When Isaiah says, "He hath anointed me,"

he thereby means that Jesus is the Christ and that Christ should do all these works, and he who is doing them must be the Christ. For the Greek word Christ is Messiah in Hebrew, Unctus in Latin, and Gesalbter (anointed) in German. But the kings and priests were usually anointed for the kingdom and priesthood. But this anointed king and priest, Isaiah says, shall be anointed by God himself, not with real oil, but with the Holy Spirit that should come upon him, saying, "The Spirit of the Lord Jehovah is upon me." That is my anointment with which the Spirit anointed me. Thus he indeed preaches good tidings to the weak, gives sight to the blind, heals all kinds of sickness, and proclaims the acceptable year, the time of grace, etc.

Again Isaiah says, "Behold, your God will come with vengeance, with the recompense of God; he will come and save you. Then the eyes of the blind shall be opened, and the ears of the deaf shall be unstopped. Then shall the lame man leap as a hart, and the tongue of the dumb shall sing," etc., in Isaiah 35:4–5. Now, if they would compare the Scriptures with these works, and these works with the Scriptures, they would recognize John's witness by Christ's works, that he was the true Messiah. Luke says, in Luke 7:21, that Christ at that time, when John's disciples asked him, healed many of their diseases and plagues and evil spirits, and bestowed sight on many that were blind.

11. But here we must take to heart the good example of Christ in that he appeals to his works, even as the tree is known by its fruits, thus rebuking all false teachers, the pope, bishops, priests, and monks to appear in the future and shield themselves by his name, saying, "We are Christians"; just as the pope is boasting that he is the vicar of Christ. Here we have it stated that where the works are absent, there is also no Christ. Christ is a living, active, and fruit-bearing character who does not rest, but works unceasingly wherever he is. Therefore, those bishops and teachers that are not doing the works of Christ, we should avoid and consider as wolves.

12. But they say, Why, it is not necessary for everyone to do these works of Christ. How can all the pious give sight to the blind, make the lame walk, and do other miracles like those of Christ? Answer: Christ did also other works; he exercised himself in patience, love, peace, meekness, etc. This, everybody should do. Do these works, and then we also shall know Christ by his works.

13. Here they reply, Christ says, "The scribes and the Pharisees sit on Moses' seat; all things therefore whatsoever they bid you, these do and observe; but do not ye after their works; for they say, and do not," in Matthew 23:2–3. Here Christ commanded to judge the doctrine but not the life. Answer: What do I hear? Have you now become Pharisees and hypocrites, and confess it yourselves? If we would say this about you then you would indeed become angry.

Be it so, if you are such hypocrites and apply these words of Christ to yourselves, then you must also apply to yourselves all the other words Christ speaks
against the Pharisees. However, as they wish to shield themselves by these
words of Christ and put to silence the ignorant, we will further consider the
same, inasmuch as the murderers of Christians at the Council of Constance
also attacked John Huss with this passage, claiming that it granted them liberty
for their tyranny, so that no one dared to oppose their doctrine.

14. It must, therefore, be observed that teaching is also a work, yea, even
the chief work of Christ, because here among his works he mentions that
to the poor the Gospel is preached. Therefore, just as the tyrants are known
by their works, so are they known by their teachings. Where Christ is, there
surely the Gospel will be preached; but where the Gospel is not preached,
there Christ is not present.

15. Now in order to grant our Pharisees that not the life but the doctrine
should be judged, be it so, let them teach, and we will gladly spare their lives;
but then they are a great deal worse than the Pharisees who taught Moses'
doctrine, though they did not practice it. But our blockheads are idols; there
is neither letting nor doing, neither life nor doctrine. They sit on Christ's seat
and teach their own lies and silence the Gospel. Hence this passage of Christ
will not shield them; they must be wolves and murderers as Christ calls them,
in John 10:1.

16. Thus Christ here wants them to hear the Pharisees but only on Moses'
seat, that is, if they taught the law of Moses, the commandments of God.

In the same place Christ forbids to do according to their works, he mentions their teachings among their works, saying, "Yea, they bind heavy burdens and grievous to be borne, and lay them on men's shoulders; but they
themselves will not move them with their finger," in Matthew 23:4. Observe
here that Christ first of all forbids among their works their teachings grievous
to be borne, as being of chief import, so that finally the meaning of the passage is, All that they teach according to Moses, you should keep and do, but
whatever they teach and do besides, you should not observe. Even so should
we listen to our Pharisees on Christ's seat only when they preach the Gospel
to the poor, and not hear them nor do what they otherwise teach or do.

17. Thus you perceive how skillfully the rude papists made this passage
the foundation of their doctrine, lies, and tyranny, though no other passage
is more strongly against them and more severely condemns their teachings
than this one. Christ's words stand firm and are clear; do not follow their
works. But their doctrine is their own work, and not God's. They are a people
exalted only to lie and to pervert the Scriptures. Moreover, if one's life is bad,

it would be strange indeed if he should preach right; he would always have to preach against himself, which he will hardly do without additions and foreign doctrines. In short, he who does not preach the Gospel identifies himself as one who is sitting neither on Moses' nor on Christ's seat. For this reason you should do neither according to his words nor according to his works, but flee from him as Christ's sheep do, in John 10:4–5, "And the sheep follow him, for they know his voice. And a stranger will they not follow, but flee from him." But if you wish to know what their seat is called, then listen to David, "Blessed is the man that walketh not in the counsel of the wicked, nor standeth in the way of the sinner, nor sitteth in the seat of scoffers, in Psalm 1:1. Again, in Psalm 94:20, "Shall the throne of wickedness have fellowship with thee, which frameth mischief by statute?"

18. But what does it mean when Christ says, "The poor have good tidings preached to them"? Is it not preached also to the rich and to the whole world? Again, why is the Gospel so great a thing, so great a blessing as Christ teaches, seeing that so many people despise and oppose it? Here we must know what Gospel really is, otherwise we cannot understand this passage. We must, therefore, diligently observe that from the beginning God has sent into the world a twofold Word, or message: the Law and the Gospel. These two messages must be rightly distinguished, one from the other, and properly understood for, besides the Scriptures, there never has been a book written to this day, not even by a saint, in which these two messages, the Law and the Gospel, have been properly explained and distinguished, and yet so very much depends on such an explanation.

The Difference Between the Law and the Gospel

19. The law is that Word by which God teaches what we shall do as, for instance, the Ten Commandments. Now, if human nature is not aided by God's grace, it is impossible to keep the law, for the reason that man, since the fall of Adam in paradise, is depraved and full of sinful desires, so that he cannot from his heart's desire find pleasure in the law, which fact we all experience in ourselves. For no one lives who does not prefer that there were no law, and everyone feels and knows in himself that it is difficult to lead a pious life and do good and, on the other hand, that it is easy to lead a wicked life and to do evil. But this difficulty or unwillingness to do the good is the reason we do not keep the law of God. For whatever is done with aversion and unwillingness is considered by God as not done at all. Thus the law of God convicts us, even by our own experience, that by nature we are evil, disobedient, lovers of sin, and hostile to God's laws.

20. From all this, either self-confidence or despair must follow. Self-confidence follows when a man strives to fulfill the law by his own good works, by trying hard to do as the words of the law command. He serves God, he swears not, he honors father and mother, he kills not, he does not commit adultery, etc. But meanwhile he does not look into his heart, does not realize with what motives he leads a good life, and conceals the old Adam in his heart. For if he would truly examine his heart, he would realize that he is doing all unwillingly and with compulsion, that he fears hell or seeks heaven, if he be not prompted by things of less importance, as honor, goods, health, and fear of being humiliated, of being punished or of being visited by a plague. In short, he would have to confess that he would rather lead a wicked life if it were not that he fears the consequences, for the law only restrains him. But because he does not realize his bad motives, he lives securely, looks only at his outward works and not into his heart, prides himself on keeping the law of God perfectly, and thus the countenance of Moses remains covered to him, that is, he does not understand the meaning of the law, namely, that it must be kept with a happy, free, and willing mind.

21. Just as an immoral person, if you should ask him why he commits adultery, can answer only that he is doing it for the sake of the carnal pleasure he finds in it. For he does not do it for reward or punishment, he expects no gain from it, nor does he hope to escape from the evil of it. Such willingness the law requires in us, so that if you should ask a virtuous man why he leads a chaste life, he would answer, Not for the sake of heaven or hell, honor or disgrace, but for the sole reason that he considers it honorable, and that it pleases him exceedingly, even if it were not commanded. Behold, such a heart delights in God's law and keeps it with pleasure. Such people love God and righteousness, they hate and fear naught but unrighteousness. However, no one is thus by nature. The unrighteous love reward and profit, fear and hate punishment and pain; therefore, they also hate God and righteousness, love themselves and unrighteousness. They are hypocrites, disguisers, deceivers, liars, and self-conceited. So are all men without grace, but above all, the saints who rely on their good works. For this reason, the Scriptures conclude, "All men are liars," in Psalm 116:11; "Every man at his best estate is altogether vanity," in Psalm 39:5; and "There is none that doeth good, no, not one," in Psalm 14:3.

22. Despair follows when man becomes conscious of his evil motives, and realizes that it is impossible for him to love the law of God, finding nothing good in himself; but only hatred of the good and delight in doing evil. Now he realizes that the law cannot be kept only by works, hence he despairs of his works and does not rely upon them. He should have love but he finds

none, nor can have any through his own efforts or out of his own heart. Now he must be a poor, miserable, and humiliated spirit whose conscience is burdened and in anguish because of the law, commanding and demanding payment in full when he does not possess even a farthing with which to pay. Only to such persons is the law beneficial, because it has been given for the purpose of working such knowledge and humiliation; that is its real mission. These persons well know how to judge the works of hypocrites and fraudulent saints, namely, as nothing but lies and deception. David referred to this when he said, "I said in my haste, all men are liars," in Psalm 116:11.

23. For this reason, Paul calls the law a law unto death, saying, "And the commandment, which was unto life, this I found to be unto death," in Romans 7:10; and a power of sin. In 1 Corinthians 15:56, "And the power of sin is the law," and in 2 Corinthians 3:6, he says, "For the letter killeth, but the spirit giveth life." All this means, if the law and human nature be brought into a right relation, the one to the other, then will sin and a troubled conscience first become manifest. Man, then, sees how desperately wicked his heart is, how great his sins are, even as to things he formerly considered good works and no sin. He now is compelled to confess that by and of himself he is a child of perdition, a child of God's wrath and of hell. Then there is only fear and trembling, all self-conceit vanishes, while fear and despair fill his heart. Thus man is crushed and put to naught, and truly humbled.

Inasmuch as all this is caused only by the law, Saint Paul truly says, that it is a law unto death and a letter that killeth, and that through the commandment sin becomes exceedingly sinful, in Romans 7:13, provoking God's wrath. For the law gives and helps us in no way whatever; it only demands and drives and shows us our misery and depravity.

Concerning the Gospel

24. The other Word of God is neither law nor commandments, and demands nothing of us. But when that has been done by the first word, namely, the law, and has worked deep despair and wretchedness in our hearts, then God comes and offers us his blessed and life-giving word and promises; he pledges and obligates himself to grant grace and help in order to deliver us from misery, not only to pardon all our sins, but even to blot them out, and in addition to this to create in us love and delight in keeping his law.

25. Behold, this divine promise of grace and forgiveness of sin is rightly called the Gospel. And I say here, again, that by the Gospel you must by no means understand anything else than the divine promise of God's grace and his forgiveness of sin. For thus it was that Paul's Epistles were never

understood, nor can they be understood by the papists, because they do not know what the law and the Gospel really mean. They hold Christ to be a lawmaker, and the Gospel a mere doctrine of a new law. That is nothing else than locking up the Gospel and entirely concealing it.

26. Now, the word Gospel is of Greek origin and signifies in German *Frohliche Botschaft*, that is, glad tidings, because it proclaims the blessed doctrine of life eternal by divine promise, and offers grace and forgiveness of sin. Therefore, works do not belong to the Gospel, as it is not a law; only faith belongs to it, as it is altogether a promise and an offer of divine grace. Whosoever now believes the Gospel will receive grace and the Holy Spirit. This will cause the heart to rejoice and find delight in God, and will enable the believer to keep the law cheerfully, without expecting reward, without fear of punishment, without seeking compensation, as the heart is perfectly satisfied with God's grace, by which the law has been fulfilled.

27. But all these promises from the beginning are founded on Christ, so that God promises no one this grace except through Christ, who is the messenger of the divine promise to the whole world. For this reason he came and through the Gospel brought these promises into all the world, which before this time had been proclaimed by the prophets. It is, therefore, in vain if anyone, like the Jews, expects the fulfillment of the divine promises without Christ. All is centered and decreed in Christ. Whosoever will not hear him shall have no promises of God. For just as God acknowledges no law besides the law of Moses and the writings of the prophets, so he makes no promises except through Christ alone.

28. But, you may reply, is there not also much law in the Gospel and in the Epistles of Paul? and, again, many promises in the writings of Moses and the prophets? Answer: There is no book in the Bible in which both are not found. God has always placed side by side both law and promise. For he teaches by the law what we are to do and, by the promises, whence we shall receive power to do it.

29. But the New Testament especially is called the Gospel above the other books of the Bible because it was written after the coming of Christ, who fulfilled the divine promises, brought them unto us, and publicly proclaimed them by oral preaching, which promises were before concealed in the Old Testament Scriptures. Therefore, hold to this distinction, and no matter what books you have before you, be they of the Old or of the New Testament, read them with a discrimination so as to observe that when promises are made in a book, it is a Gospel book; when commandments are given, it is a law book. But because in the New Testament the promises are found so abundantly, and

in the Old Testament so many laws, the former is called the Gospel, and the latter the Book of the Law. We now come back to our text.

"And the poor have good tidings preached unto them."

30. From what has just been said, it is easily understood that among the works of Christ none is greater than preaching the Gospel to the poor. This means nothing else than that to the poor the divine promise of grace and consolation in and through Christ is preached, offered, and presented, so that to him who believes all his sins are forgiven, the law is fulfilled, conscience is appeased, and, at last, life eternal is bestowed upon him. What more joyful tidings could a poor sorrowful heart and a troubled conscience hear than this? How could the heart become more bold and courageous than by such consoling, blissful words of promise? Sin, death, hell, the world and the devil, and every evil are scorned when a poor heart receives and believes this consolation of the divine promise. To give sight to the blind and to raise up the dead are but insignificant deeds compared with preaching the Gospel to the poor. Therefore, Christ mentions it as the greatest and best among these works.

31. But it must be observed that Christ says the Gospel is preached to none but to the poor only, thus without doubt intending it to be a message for the poor only. For it has always been preached unto the whole world, as Christ says, "Go ye into all the world, and preach the Gospel to the whole creation," in Mark 16:15. Surely these poor are not the beggars and the bodily poor, but the spiritually poor, namely, those who do not covet and love earthly goods; yes, rather those poor, broken-hearted ones who in the agony of their conscience seek and desire help and consolation so ardently that they covet neither riches nor honor. Nothing will be of help to them, unless they have a merciful God. Here is true spiritual weakness. They are those for whom such a message is intended, and in their hearts they are delighted with it. They feel they have been delivered from hell and death.

32. Therefore, though the Gospel is heard by all the world, yet it is not accepted but by the poor only. Moreover, it is to be preached and proclaimed to all the world, that it is a message only for the poor, and that the rich men cannot receive it. Whosoever would receive it must first become poor, as Christ says, in Matthew 9:13, that he came not to call the righteous but only sinners, although he called all the world. But his calling was such that he desired to be accepted only by sinners, and all he called should become sinners. This they resented. In like manner, all should become poor who heard the Gospel, that they might be worthy of the Gospel; but this they also resented. Therefore, the Gospel remained only for the poor. Thus God's grace was also

preached before all the world to the humble, in order that all might become humble, but they would not be humble.

33. Hence you see who are the greatest enemies of the Gospel, namely, the work-righteous saints, who are self-conceited, as has been said before. For the Gospel has not the least in common with them. They want to be rich in works, but the Gospel wills that they are to become poor. They will not yield, neither can the Gospel yield, as it is the unchangeable Word of God. Thus they and the Gospel clash, one with another, as Christ says, "And he that falleth on this stone shall be broken to pieces; but on whomsoever it shall fall, it will scatter him as dust," in Matthew 21:44.

Again, they condemn the Gospel as being error and heresy; and we observe it comes to pass daily, as it has from the beginning of the world, that between the Gospel and the work-righteous saints there is no peace, no good will, and no reconciliation. But meanwhile Christ must suffer himself to be crucified anew, for he and those that are his must place themselves, as it were, into this vise, namely, between the Gospel and the work-righteous saints, and thus be pressed and crushed like the wheat between the upper and nether millstones. But the lower stone is the quiet, peaceable, and immovable Gospel, while the upper stone is the works and their masters, who are ranting and raging.

34. With all this John contradicts strongly the fleshly and worldly opinion his disciples entertained concerning Christ's coming. They thought that the great king, whom John extolled so highly, namely, that the latchet of whose shoe he was not worthy to unloose, in John 1:27, would enter in such splendor that everything would be gold and costly ornaments, and immediately the streets would be spread with pearls and silks. As they lifted up their eyes so high and looked for such splendor, Christ turns their look downward and holds before them the blind, lame, deaf, dumb, poor, and everything that conflicts with such splendor, and contrariwise he presents himself in the state of a common servant rather than that of a great king, whose shoe's latchet John considered himself unworthy to unloose, as though Christ would say to them, "Banish your high expectations, look not to my person and state, but to the works I do. Worldly lords, because they rule by force, must be accompanied by rich, high, healthy, strong, wise, and able men. With them they have to associate, and they need them, or their kingdom could not exist; hence they can never attend to the blind, lame, deaf, dumb, dead, lepers, and the poor.

But my kingdom, because it seeks not its own advantage, but rather bestows benefits upon others, is sufficient of itself and needs no one's help; therefore, I cannot bear to be surrounded by such as are already sufficient of themselves, such as are healthy, rich, strong, pure, active, pious, and able in every respect. To such, I am of no benefit; they obtain nothing from me. Yea, they would be a disgrace to me, because it would seem that I needed them and were benefited by them, as worldly rulers are by their subjects. Therefore, I must do otherwise and keep to those who can become partakers of me, and I must associate with the blind, the lame, the dumb, and all kinds of afflicted ones. This the character and nature of my kingdom demand. For this reason, I must appear in a way that such people can feel at home in my company.

35. And now very aptly follow the words, "And blessed is he, whosoever shall find no occasion of stumbling in me." Why? Because Christ's humble appearance and John's excellent testimony of Christ seemed to disagree with each other. Human reason could not make them rhyme. Now all the Scriptures pointed to Christ, and there was danger of misinterpreting them. Reason spoke thus, Can this be the Christ, of whom all the Scriptures speak? Should he be the one, whose shoe's latchet John thought himself unworthy to unloose, though I scarcely consider him worthy to clean my shoes? Therefore, it is surely true that it is a great blessing not to find occasion of stumbling in Christ, and there is here no other help or remedy than to look at his works and compare them with the Scriptures. Otherwise, it is impossible to keep from being offended at Christ.

Two Kinds of Offenses

36. Here you observe that there are two kinds of offenses, one of doctrine and the other of life. These two offenses must be carefully considered. The offense of doctrine comes when one believes, teaches, or thinks of Christ in a different way than he should, as the Jews here thought of and taught Christ to be different than he really was, expecting him to be a temporal king. Of this offense the Scriptures treat mostly. Christ and Paul always dwell upon it, scarcely mentioning any other. Note well, that Christ and Paul speak of this offense.

37. It is not without reason that men are admonished faithfully to remember this. For under the reign of the pope this offense has been hushed entirely, so that neither monk nor priest knows of any other offense than that caused by open sin and wicked living, which the Scripture does not call an offense; yet they thus construe and twist this word.

On the contrary, all their doings and all their teachings by which they think to benefit the world, they do not consider to be an offense, but a great help; and yet these are dangerous offenses, the like of which never before existed. For they teach the people to believe that the Mass is an offering and a good work, that by works men may become pious, may atone for sin and be saved, all of which is nothing else than rejecting Christ and destroying faith.

38. Thus the world today is filled with offenses up to the very heavens, so that it is terrible to think of it. For no one now seeks Christ among the poor, the blind, the dead, etc.; but all expect to enter heaven in a different way, which expectation must surely fail.

39. The offense of life is, when one sees an openly wicked work done by another and teaches it. But it is impossible to avoid this offense, inasmuch as we have to live among the wicked, nor is it so dangerous, since everybody knows that such offense is sinful, and no one is deceived by it, but intentionally follows the known evil. There is neither disguise nor deception. But the offense of doctrine is that there should be the most beautiful religious ceremonies, the noblest works, the most honorable life, and that it is impossible for common reason to censure or discern it; only faith knows through the spirit that it is all wrong. Against this offense Christ warns us, saying, "But whoso shall cause one of these little ones that believe on me to stumble, it is profitable for him that a great millstone should be hanged about his neck, and that he should be sunk in the depth of the sea," in Matthew 18:6.

40. Whosoever does not preach Christ, or who preaches him otherwise than as one caring for the blind, the lame, the dead, and the poor, like the Gospel teaches, let us flee from him as from the devil himself, because he teaches us how to become unhappy and to stumble in Christ; as it is now done by the pope, the monks, and the teachers in their high schools. All their doings are an offense from head to foot, from the skin to the marrow, so that the snow is scarcely anything but water; nor can these things exist without causing great offense, inasmuch as offense is the nature and essence of their doings. Therefore, to undertake to reform the pope, the convents, and the high schools and still maintain them in their essence and character, would be like squeezing water out of snow and still preserving the snow. But what it means to preach Christ among the poor, we shall see at the end of our text.

III. HOW AND WHY CHRIST PRAISES JOHN

And as these went their way, Jesus began to say unto the multitudes concerning John, "What went ye out into the wilderness to behold? a reed shaken by the wind? But what went ye out to see? a man clothed in soft raiments? Behold, they that wear soft raiment are in kings' houses.
But wherefore went ye out? to see a prophet? Yea, I say unto you, and much more than a prophet."

41. Inasmuch as Christ thus lauds John the Baptist, because he is not a reed, nor clothed in soft raiment, and because he is more than a prophet, he gives us

to understand by these figurative words, that the people were inclined to look upon John as a reed, as clad in soft raiment, and as a prophet. Therefore we must see what he means by them, and why he censures and rejects these opinions of theirs. Enough has been said, that John bore witness of Christ in order that the people might not take offense at Christ's humble appearance and manner.

42. Now, as it was of great importance for them to believe John's witness and acknowledge Christ, he praised John first for his steadfastness, thus rebuking their wavering on account of which they would not believe John's witness. It is as though he would say, You have heard John's witness concerning me, but now you do not adhere to it, you take offense at me and your hearts are wavering; you are looking for another, but know not who, nor when and where, and thus your hearts are like a reed shaken by the wind to and fro; you are sure of nothing, and would rather hear something else than the truth about me. Now do you think that John should also turn his witness from me and, as is the case with your thoughts, turn it to the winds and speak of another whom you would be pleased to hear? Not so. John does not waver, nor does his witness fluctuate; he does not follow your swaying delusion; but you must stay your wavering by his witness and thus adhere to me and expect none other.

43. Again, Christ lauds John because of his coarse raiment, as though to say, Perhaps you might believe him when he says that I am he that should come as to my person; but you expect him to speak differently about me, saying something smooth and agreeable, that would be pleasant to hear. It is indeed hard and severe that I come so poor and despised. You desire me to rush forth with pomp and flourish of trumpets. Had John thus spoken of me, then he would not appear so coarse and severe himself. But do not think thus. Whoever desires to preach about me must not preach different than John is doing. It's to no purpose; I will assume no other state and manner. Those who teach different than John are not in the wilderness but in kings' houses. They are rich and honored by the people. They are teachers of man-made doctrines, teaching themselves and not me.

44. Christ lauds John, thirdly, because of the dignity of his office, namely, that he is not only a prophet, but even more than a prophet, as though to say, In your high-soaring, fluctuating opinion, you take John for a prophet who speaks of the coming of Christ, just as the other prophets have done, and thus again your thoughts go beyond me to a different time when you expect Christ to come, according to John's witness, so that you will in no case accept me. But I say to you, your thoughts are wrong. For just as John warns you not to be like a shaken reed, and not to look for any other than myself, nor to expect me in a different state and manner from that in which you see me, he

also forbids you to look for another time, because his witness points to this person of mine, to this state and manner, and to this time, and it opposes your fickle ideas in every way and binds you firmly to my person.

45. Now, if you want to do John justice, then you must simply accept his witness and believe that this is the person, the state and manner, and the time that you should accept, and abandon your presumption and your waiting for another person, state, and time. For it is decreed that John should be no shaken reed, not a man of soft raiment and, above all, not a prophet pointing to future times, but a messenger of present events. He will not write as did the prophets, but will point out and orally announce him who has been predicted by the prophets, saying,

> *"This is he, of whom it is written, 'Behold, I send my messenger*
> *before thy face, who shall prepare the way before thee.'"*

46. What else can this mean than that you dare not wait for another, neither for another manner of mine, neither for another time. Here I am present, the one of whom John speaks. For John is not a prophet but a messenger. And not a messenger that is sent by the master who stays at home, but a messenger that goes before the face of his master and brings the master along with him, so that there is but one time for the messenger and for the master. Now if you do not accept John as such a messenger but take him for a prophet who only proclaims the coming of the Lord, as the other prophets have done, then you will fail to understand me, the Scriptures, and everything else.

47. Thus we see Christ pleads, mainly for them to take John as a messenger and not as a prophet. To this end, Christ quotes the Scriptures referring to the passage in Malachi 3:1, "Behold, I send my messenger, and he shall prepare the way before me," which he does not do in reference to the other points, namely, his person and manner. For to this day, it is the delusion of the Jews that they look for another time; and if they then had believed that the time was at hand and had considered John a messenger and not a prophet, then everything could easily have been adjusted as to the person and manner of Christ, inasmuch as they at last had to accept his person and manner, at least after the expired time. For there should be no other time than the days of John, the messenger and preparer of the way for his Master. But as they do not heed the time, and look for another time, it is scarcely possible to convince them by his person and manner. They remain shaken reeds and soft-raiment seekers as long as they take John for his prophet and not for his messenger.

48. We must accustom ourselves to the Scriptures, in which angel (angelus) really means a messenger, not a bearer of messages or one who carries

letters, but one who is sent to solicit orally for the message. Hence in the Scriptures this name is common to all messengers of God in heaven and on earth, be they holy angels in heaven or the prophets and apostles on earth. For thus Malachi speaks of the office of the priest, "For the priest's lips should keep knowledge, and they should seek the law at his mouth; for he is the messenger (angel) of Jehovah of hosts," in Malachi 2:7. Again, "Then spake Haggai, Jehovah's messenger (angel) in Jehovah's message unto the people," in Haggai 1:13. And again, "And it came to pass, when the days were well nigh come that he should be received up, he steadfastly set his face to go to Jerusalem, and sent messengers (angels) before his face," in Luke 9:51.

Thus they are called God's angels or messengers and solicitors, who proclaim his Word. From this is also derived the word Gospel, which means good tidings. But the heavenly spirits are called angels chiefly because they are the highest and most exalted messengers of God.

49. Thus John is also an angel or Word-messenger, and not only such a messenger, but one who also prepares the way before the face of the Master in a manner that the Master himself follows him immediately, which no prophet ever did. For this reason, John is more than a prophet, namely, an angel or messenger, and a forerunner, so that in his day the Lord of all the prophets himself comes with this messenger.

50. The preparing here means to make ready the way, to put out of the way all that interferes with the course of the Lord, just as the servant clears the way before the face of his master by removing wood, stones, people, and all that is in the way. But what was it that blocked the way of Christ and John was to remove? Sin, without doubt, especially the good works of the haughty saints; that is, he should make known to everybody that the works and deeds of all men are sin and iniquity, and that all need the grace of Christ. He who knows and acknowledges this thoroughly is himself humble and has well prepared the way for Christ. Of this we shall speak in the following Gospel. Now is the opportunity for us to receive a blessing from this Gospel lesson.

IV. THE APPLICATION OF THIS GOSPEL

The Doctrine of Faith and Good Works

51. As we have said touching the other Gospels, that we should learn from them the two doctrines of faith and love, or accepting and bestowing good works, so we should do here, extol faith and exercise love. Faith receives the good works of Christ; love bestows good works on our neighbor.

52. In the first place, our faith is strengthened and increased when Christ is held forth to us in his own natural works, namely, that he associates only with the blind, the deaf, the lame, the lepers, the dead, and the poor; that is, in pure love and kindness toward all who are in need and in misery, so that finally Christ is nothing else than consolation and a refuge for all the distressed and troubled in conscience. Here is necessary faith that trusts in the Gospel and relies upon it, never doubting that Christ is just as he is presented to us in this Gospel, and does not think of him otherwise, nor let anyone persuade us to believe otherwise. Then surely we learn Christ as we believe and as this Gospel speaks of him. For as you believe, so you will have it And blessed is he who finds here no occasion of stumbling in Christ.

53. Here you must with all diligence beware of taking offense. Who stumble at Christ? All that teach you to do works instead of teaching you to believe. Those who hold forth Christ to you as a lawmaker and a judge, and refuse to let Christ be a helper and a comforter, torment you by putting works before and in the way of God in order to atone for your sins and to merit grace. Such are the teachings of the pope, priests, monks, and their high schools, who with their masses and religious ceremonies cause you to open your eyes and mouth in astonishment, leading you to another Christ and withholding from you the real Christ. For if you desire to believe rightly and to possess Christ truly, then you must reject all works that you intend to place before and in the way of God. They are only stumbling blocks, leading you away from Christ and from God. Before God no works are acceptable but Christ's own works. Let these plead for you before God, and do no other work before him than to believe that Christ is doing his works for you and is placing them before God in your behalf.

In order to keep your faith pure, do nothing else than stand still, enjoy its blessings, accept Christ's works, and let him bestow his love upon you. You must be blind, lame, deaf, dead, leprous, and poor; otherwise, you will stumble at Christ. That Gospel which suffers Christ to be seen and to be doing good only among the needy will not belie you.

54. This means to acknowledge Christ aright and to embrace him. This is true and Christian believing. But those who intend to atone for sins and to become pious by their own works will miss the present Christ and look for another, or at least they will believe that he should do otherwise, that first of all he should come and accept their works and consider them pious. These are, like the Jews, lost forever. There is no help for them.

55. In the second place, Christ teaches us rightly to apply the works and shows us what good works are. All other work, except faith, we should apply

to our neighbor. For God demands of us no other work that we should do for him than to exercise faith in Christ. With that he is satisfied, and with that we give honor to him, as to one who is merciful, long-suffering, wise, kind, truthful, and the like. After this, think of nothing else than to do to your neighbor as Christ has done to you, and let all your works together with all your life be applied to your neighbor. Look for the poor, sick, and all kinds of needy, help them and let your life's energy here appear, so that they may enjoy your kindness, helping whoever needs you, as much as you possibly can with your life, property, and honor. Whoever points you to other good works than these, avoid him as a wolf and as Satan, because he wants to put a stumbling block in your way, as David says, "In the way wherein I walk have they hidden a snare for me," in Psalm 142:3.

56. But this is done by the perverted, misguided people of the papists, who, with their religious ceremonies, set aside such Christian works, and teach the people to serve God only and not also mankind. They establish convents, masses, vigils, become religious, do this and that. And these poor, blind people call that serving God, which they have chosen themselves. But know that to serve God is nothing else than to serve your neighbor and do good to him in love, be it a child, wife, servant, enemy, friend; without making any difference, whoever needs your help in body or soul, and wherever you can help in temporal or spiritual matters. This is serving God and doing good works. O Lord God, how do we fools live in this world, neglecting to do such works, though in all parts of the world we find the needy, on whom we could bestow our good works; but no one looks after them nor cares for them. But look to your own life. If you do not find yourself among the needy and the poor, where the Gospel shows us Christ, then you may know that your faith is not right and that you have not yet tasted of Christ's benevolence and work for you.

57. Therefore, behold what an important saying it is, "Blessed is he, whosoever shall find no occasion of stumbling in me." We stumble in two respects. In faith, because we expect to become pious Christians in a different way than through Christ, and go our way blindly, not acknowledging Christ. In love we stumble, because we are not mindful of the poor and needy, do not look after them, and yet we think we satisfy the demands of faith with other works than these. Thus we come under the judgment of Christ, who says, "For I was hungry, and ye did not give me to eat, I was thirsty, and yet ye gave me no drink," in Matthew 25:42. Again, "Inasmuch as ye did it not unto one of these least, ye did it not unto me," in Matthew 25:45.

Why is this judgment right, if not for the reason that we do not unto our neighbor as Christ has done to us? He has bestowed on us needy ones his great, rich, eternal blessings, but we will not bestow our meager service on our neighbors, thus showing that we do not truly believe, and that we have neither accepted nor tasted his blessings. Many will say, "Did we not do wonders in thy name, did we not speak and cast out devils?" But he will answer them, "Depart from me, ye that work iniquity," in Matthew 7:23, and why? Because they did not retain their true Christian faith and love.

58. Thus we see in this Gospel how difficult it is to acknowledge Christ. There is a stumbling block in the way, and one takes offense at this, another at that. There is no headway, not even with the disciples of John, though they plainly see Christ's works and hear his words.

59. This we also do. Though we see, hear, understand, and must confess that Christian life is faith in God and love to our needy neighbor, yet there is no progress. This one clings to his religious ceremonies and his own works, that one is scraping all to himself and helps no one. Even those who gladly hear and understand the doctrine of pure faith do not proceed to serve their neighbor, as though they expected to be saved by faith without works; they see not that their faith is not faith, but a shadow of faith, just as the picture in the mirror is not the face itself, but only a reflection of the same, as Saint James so beautifully writes, saying, "But be ye doers of the Word, and not hearers only, deluding your own selves. For if anyone is a hearer of the Word and not a doer, he is like unto a man beholding his natural face in a mirror: for he beholdeth himself, and goeth away, and straightway forgetteth what manner of man he was," in James 1:22–25. So also there within themselves many behold a reflection of true faith when they hear and speak of the Word, but as soon as the hearing and speaking are done, they are concerned about other affairs and are not doing according to it, and thus they always forget about the fruit of faith, namely, Christian love, of which Paul also says, "For the kingdom of God is not in word, but in power," in 1 Corinthians 4:20.

The Fourth Sunday in Advent

❧

The Witness and Confession of John the Baptist

And this is the witness of John, when the Jews sent unto him from Jerusalem priests and Levites to ask him, "Who art thou?" And he confessed, and denied not; and he confessed, "I am not the Christ." And they asked him, "What then? Art thou Elijah?" And he saith, "I am not." "Art thou the prophet?" And he answered, "No." They said therefore unto him, "Who art thou? that we may give an answer to them that sent us. What sayest thou of thyself?" He said, "I am the voice of one crying in the wilderness, 'Make straight the way of the Lord,' as said Isaiah the prophet." And they had been sent from the Pharisees. And they asked him, and said unto him, "Why then baptizest thou, if thou art not the Christ, neither Elijah, neither the prophet?" John answered them, saying, "I baptize with water: in the midst of you standeth one whom ye know not, even he that cometh after me, the latchet of whose shoe I am not worthy to unloose." These things were done in Bethany beyond the Jordan, where John was baptizing. — JOHN 1:19–28

I. THE WITNESS AND CONFESSION OF JOHN THE BAPTIST

1. With many words the evangelist describes and magnifies the testimony of John. Although it would have been sufficient if he had written of him, "He confessed," he repeats it and says, "He confessed and denied not." This was surely done in order to extol the beautiful constancy of John in a sore trial, when he was tempted to a flagrant denial of the truth. And now consider the particular circumstances.

2. First, there are sent to him not servants or ordinary citizens, but priests and Levites from the highest and noblest class, who were Pharisees, that is to say, the leaders of the people. Surely a distinguished embassy for a common man, who might justly have felt proud of such an honor, for the favor of lords and princes is highly esteemed in this world.

3. Secondly, they sent to him not common people, but citizens of Jerusalem, to wit, the capital, the Sanhedrin, and the leaders of the Jewish nation. So it was as if the entire people came and did honor to him. What a wind that was! and how he might have been inflated had he possessed a vain and worldly heart!

4. Thirdly, they do not offer him a present, nor ordinary glory, but the highest glory of all, the kingdom and all authority, being ready to accept him as the Christ. Surely a mighty and sweet temptation! For, had he not perceived that they wished to regard him as the Christ, he would not have said, "I am not the Christ." And Luke, in Luke 3:15–16, also writes that, when everybody thought he was the Christ, John spoke, "I am not he who you think I am, but I am being sent before him."

5. Fourthly, when he would not accept this honor, they tried him with another and were ready to take him for Elijah. For they had a prophecy in the last chapter of the prophet Malachi, where God says, "Behold, I will send you Elijah the prophet, before the coming of the great and dreadful day of the Lord; and he shall turn the heart of the fathers to the children, and the heart of the children to the fathers, lest I come and smite the earth with a curse."

6. Fifthly, seeing that he would not be Elijah, they go on tempting him and offer him the homage due to an ordinary prophet, for since Malachi they had not had a prophet. John, however, remains firm and unshaken, although tried by the offer of so much honor.

7. Sixthly and lastly, not knowing of any more honors, they left him to choose as to who or what he wished to be regarded, for they greatly desired to do him homage. But John will have none of this honor and gives only this for an answer, that he is a voice calling to them and to everybody. This they do not heed. What all this means, we shall hear later on. Let us now examine the text.

And this is the witness of John, when the Jews sent unto him from Jerusalem priests and Levites to ask him, "Who art thou?"

8. They sent to him, why did they not come themselves? John had come to preach repentance to the entire Jewish people. This preaching of John they did not heed; it is clear, therefore, that they did not send to him with good and pure intentions, offering him such honor. Neither did they truly believe him to be the Christ, or Elijah, or a prophet; otherwise, they would have come themselves to be baptized, as did the others. What then did they seek of him? Christ explains this, in John 5:33–35, "Ye have sent unto John, and he hath borne witness unto the truth. He was the lamp that burneth and shineth, and ye were willing to rejoice for a season in his light." From these words it

is clear they looked for their own honor in John, desiring to make use of his light, his illustrious and famous name, in order to adorn themselves before the people. For if John had joined them and accepted their proffered honor, they also would have become great and glorious before all the people, as being worthy of the friendship and reverence of so holy and great a man. But would not hereby all their avarice, tyranny, and rascality have been confirmed and declared holy and worthy? Thus John, with all his holiness, would have become a sponsor for vice; and the coming of Christ would justly have been regarded with suspicion, as being opposed to the doings of the priests and tyrants, with whom John, this great and holy man, would have taken sides.

9. Thus we see what rascality they practice and how they tempt John to betray Christ and become a Judas Iscariot, in order that he might confirm their injustice and they might share his honor and popularity. What cunning fellows they are, thus to fish for John's honor! They offer him an apple for a kingdom, and would exchange counters for dollars. But he remained firm as a rock, as is shown by the statement:

And he confessed, and denied not; and he confessed, "I am not the Christ."

10. John's confession comprises two things: first, his confessing, and secondly, his not denying. His confessing is his declaration about Christ, when he says, "I am not the Christ." To this belongs also that he confesses to be neither Elijah nor a prophet. His not denying is declaration of what he really is, when he calls himself a voice in the wilderness, preparing the way of the Lord. Thus his confession is free and open, declaring not only what he is but also what he is not. For if someone declares what he is not, such a confession is still obscure and incomplete, since one cannot know what is really to be thought of him. But here John openly says what is to be thought of him, and what not, this giving the people a certain assurance in confessing that he is not the Christ, and not denying that he is the voice preparing his advent.

11. Yet someone might say, the evangelist contradicts himself in calling it a confession when John declares himself not to be Christ, whereas this is rather a denial, for he denies that he is Christ. To say, "Nay" is to deny, and the Jews wish him to confess that he is Christ, which he denies; yet the evangelist says that he confessed. And again, it is rather a confession when he says, "I am the voice in the wilderness." But the evangelist considers this matter and describes it as it is before God and not as the words sound and appear to men. For the Jews desired him to deny Christ and not to confess what he really was. But since he confesses what he is and firmly insists upon what he is not, his act is before God a precious confession and not a denial.

And they asked him, "What then? Art thou Elijah?"
and he saith, "I am not."

12. The Jews, as said above, had the prophecy concerning Elijah, that he was to come before the day of the Lord, in Malachi 4:5. It is therefore also among Christians a current belief that Elijah is to come before the last day. Some add Enoch, others Saint John the Evangelist. Of this we shall have something to say.

13. In the first place, all depends upon whether the prophet Malachi speaks of the second coming of the Lord on the last day, or of his first coming into flesh and through the Gospel. If he speaks of the last day, then we have certainly yet to expect Elijah; for God cannot lie. The coming of Enoch and Saint John, however, has no foundation in Scripture, and is therefore to be considered as a fable. If, on the other hand, the prophet speaks of Christ's coming in the flesh and through the Word, then assuredly Elijah is no more to be expected, but John is that same Elijah announced by Malachi.

14. I am of the opinion that Malachi spoke of no other Elijah than John, and that Elijah the Tishbite, who went up to heaven with the chariot of fire, is no more to be expected. To this opinion I am forced first and foremost by the words of the angel Gabriel, in Luke 1:17, who says to John's father, Zacharias, "And he shall go before his face in the spirit and power of Elijah, to turn the hearts of the fathers to the children, and the disobedient to walk in the wisdom of the just." With these words the angel manifestly refers to the prophecy of Malachi, adducing even the words of the prophet, who also says that Elijah is to turn the hearts of fathers to children, as cited above. Now then, if Malachi had meant another Elijah, the angel doubtless would not have applied these words to John.

15. In the second place, the Jews themselves of old understood Malachi to speak of Christ's coming into the flesh. Therefore, they here ask John whether he is Elijah, who is to come before the Christ. But they erred in thinking of the original and bodily Elijah. For the purport of the text is indeed that Elijah is to come beforehand, but not that same Elijah. We do not read, Elijah the Tishbite is to come, as the Bible calls him in 1 Kings 17:1 and 2 Kings 1:3–8, but merely Elijah, a prophet. This Gabriel, in Luke 1:17, explains as meaning, "In the spirit and power of Elijah," saying, as it were, He will be a real Elijah. Just as we now say of one who has another's manner and carriage, He is a true X.; as I may say, e.g., the pope is a real Caiaphas; John was a real Saint Paul. In the same manner does God through Malachi promise one who is to be a true Elijah, i.e., John the Baptist.

16. Yet would I not trust the interpretation of the Jews alone, were it not confirmed by Christ, in Matthew 10:10ff. When, on Mount Tabor, the disciples saw Elijah and Moses, they said to the Lord, "Why then say the scribes that Elijah must first come?" They meant to say, "You have already come; yet Elijah has not come first, but only now, after you: and was it not said that he was to come before you?" This interpretation was not rejected but confirmed by Christ, who said, "Elijah truly shall first come, and restore all things. But I say unto you that Elijah is come already; and they knew him not, but have done unto him whatsoever they listed." Then the disciples understood, says Saint Matthew, that he spoke of John the Baptist. Saint Mark likewise says, in Mark 9:13, "But I say unto you that Elijah is come, and they have done unto him whatsoever they would, even as it is written of him."

17. Now there is no other prophecy concerning Elijah's coming but this one of Malachi, and Christ himself applies it to John. Thus it has no force if someone were to object. Christ says that Elijah is to come first and restore all things, for Christ interprets his own words by saying, "But I tell you that Elijah is come," etc. He means to say, It is right and true what you have heard about Elijah, that he is to come first and restore all things; thus it is written and thus it must come to pass. But they do not know of which Elijah this is said, for he is come already. With these words, therefore, Christ confirms the Scriptures and the interpretation concerning the coming Elijah, but he rejects the false interpretation concerning an Elijah other than John.

18. Most strongly, however, does Christ assert, in Matthew 11:13ff., that no other Elijah is coming. He says, "All the prophets and the law prophesied until John. And if you will receive it, this is Elijah that is to come. He that hath ears to hear, let him hear." Here it is made clear that but one Elijah was to come. Had there been another, he would not have said, "John is Elijah who was to come," but he would have had to say, "John is one of the Elijahs," or simply, "He is Elijah." But by calling John that Elijah whom everybody expects, who, doubtless, was announced to come, he makes it sufficiently clear that the prophecy of Malachi is fulfilled in John, and that after this no other Elijah is to be expected.

19. We insist, therefore, that the Gospel, through which Christ has come into all the world, is the last message before the day of judgment; before this message and advent of Christ John came and prepared the way. And although all the prophets and the law prophesy until John, it is not allowed to apply them, neglecting John, to another Elijah who is yet to come. Thus also the prophecy of Malachi must fit the times of John. He carries the line of the prophets down to John's times and permits no one to pass by. And so we

conclude with certainty that no other Elijah is to come, and that the Gospel will endure unto the end of the world.

"Art thou the prophet?" And he answered, "No."

20. Some think the Jews here asked concerning that prophet of whom Moses writes in Deuteronomy 18:15, "The Lord thy God will raise up unto thee a prophet from the midst of thee, of thy brethren, like unto me, etc." But this passage Saint Peter in Acts 3:22, and Saint Stephen in Acts 7:37, apply to Christ himself, which is the correct interpretation. The Jews also certainly held this prophet in equal esteem with Moses, above Elijah and, therefore, understood him to be Christ. They asked John whether he was an ordinary prophet, like the others, since he was neither Christ nor Elijah. For they had had no prophet since the days of Malachi, who was the last and concluded the Old Testament with the above-mentioned prophecy concerning the coming of Elijah. John, therefore, is the nearest to and first after Malachi, who, in finishing his book, points to him. The Jews then asked whether he was one of the prophets. Christ likewise says of him, in Matthew 11:9, "Wherefore went ye out? to see a prophet? Yea, I say unto you, and much more than a prophet." And Matthew says, in Matthew 21:26, "All hold John as a prophet."

21. Now the question arises, Did John really confess the truth when he denied that he was Elijah or a prophet, whereas Christ himself called him Elijah and more than a prophet? He himself knew that he had come in the spirit and power of Elijah, and that the Scriptures called him Elijah. To say, therefore, that he did not consider himself a prophet because he was more than a prophet, is disgraceful and makes him an empty boaster. The truth of the matter is, that he simply and in a straightforward manner confessed the truth, namely, that he was not that Elijah about whom they asked, nor a prophet. For the prophets commonly led and taught the people, who sought advice and help from them. Such a one John was not and would not be, for the Lord was present, whom they were to follow and adhere to. He did not desire to draw the people to himself, but to lead them to Christ, which was needful before Christ himself came. A prophet foretells the coming of Christ. John, however, shows him present, which is not a prophet's task. Just so a priest in the bishop's presence would direct the people away from himself to the bishop, saying, "I am not priest; yonder is your priest"; but in the bishop's absence, he would rule the people in the place of the bishop.

22. John likewise directs the people away from himself to Christ. And although this is a higher and greater office than that of a prophet, yet it is not so on account of his merit but on account of the presence of his Master. And

in praising John for being more than a prophet, not his worthiness but that of his Master, who is present, is extolled. For it is customary for a servant to receive greater honor and reverence in the absence of his master than in his presence.

23. Even so the rank of a prophet is higher than that of John, although his office is greater and more immediate. For a prophet rules and leads the people, and they adhere to him; but John does no more than direct them away from himself to Christ, the present Master. Therefore, in the simplest and most straightforward manner, he denied being a prophet, although abounding in all the qualities of a prophet. This he did for the sake of the people, in order that they might not accept his testimony as the foretelling of a prophet and expect Christ in other, future times, but that they might recognize him as a forerunner and guide, and follow his guidance to the Lord, who was present. Witness the following words of the text:

> They said therefore unto him, "Who art thou? that we may give
> an answer to them that sent us. What sayest thou of thyself?" He said,
> "I am the voice of one crying in the wilderness, Make straight
> the way of the Lord, as said Isaiah the prophet."

24. This is the second part of his confession, in which he declares what he is, after having denied that he was Christ, or Elijah, or a prophet. As though he were to say, Your salvation is much too near for a prophet to be required. Do not strain your eyes so far out into the future, for the Lord of all the prophets is himself here, so that no prophet is needed. The Lord is coming this way, whose forerunner I am; he is treading on my heels. I am not prophesying of him as a seer, but crying as a courier, to make room for him as he walks along. I do not say, as the prophets, "Behold, he is to come"; but I say, "Behold, he is coming, he is here. I am not bringing word about him, but pointing to him with my finger. Did not Isaiah long ago foretell that such a crying to make room for the Lord should go before him? Such I am, and not a prophet. Therefore, step aside and make room, permit the Lord himself to walk among you bodily, and do not look for any more prophecies about him."

25. Now this is the answer which no learned, wise, and holy men can bear; therefore, John must surely be a heretic and be possessed of the devil. Only sinners and fools think him a holy, pious man, listen to his crying, and make room for the Lord, removing whatsoever obstructs his way. The others, however, throw logs, stones, and dirt in his way, aye, they even kill both the Lord and his forerunner for presuming to say such things to him. And why? John tells them to prepare the way of the Lord. That is to say, they have

not the Lord nor his way in them. What have they then? Where the Lord is not, nor his way, there must be man's own way, the devil, and all that is evil. Judge then, whether those holy wise people are not justly incensed at John, condemn his word, and finally slay both him and his Master! Shall he presume to hand such holy people over to the devil, and denounce all their doings as false, wicked, and damnable, claiming that their ways are not the Lord's ways, that they must first of all prepare the Lord's ways, and that they have lived all their holy lives in vain?

26. Yet, if he quietly wrote it on a tablet, they might still hear it in patience. But he gives utterance to it, yea, he cries it aloud, and that not in a corner, but openly under the sky, in the wilderness, before all the world, utterly disgracing before everybody those saints with all their doings and discrediting them with all the people. Thus they lose all honor and profit which their holy life formerly brought them. This certainly such pious men cannot bear, but for God's and justice's sake they cannot damn that false doctrine, in order that the poor people may not be misled and the service of God be not corrupted; aye, finally, they will have to kill John and his Master, to serve and obey God the Father.

27. This, then, is the preparation of Christ's way and John's proper office. He is to humble all the world, and proclaim that they are all sinners—lost, damned, poor, miserable, pitiable people; that there is no life, work, or rank, however holy, beautiful, and good it may appear, but is damnable unless Christ our God dwell therein, unless he work, walk, live, be, and do everything through faith in him; in short, that they all need Christ and should anxiously strive to share his grace.

Behold, where this is practiced, namely, that all man's work and life is as nothing, there you have the true crying of John in the wilderness and the pure and clear truth of Christianity, as Saint Paul shows, in Romans 3:23, "All have sinned, and fall short of the glory of God." This is truly to humiliate man, to cut out and annihilate his presumption. Aye, this is indeed to prepare the way of the Lord, to give room and to make way.

28. Now here are found two kinds of people: some believe the crying of John and confess it to be what he says. These are the people to whom the Lord comes, in them his way is prepared and made even, as Saint Peter says, in 1 Peter 5:5, "God giveth grace to the humble"; and the Lord himself says, in Luke 18:14, "He that humbleth himself shall be exalted." You must here diligently learn, and understand spiritually, what the way of the Lord is, how it is prepared, and what prevents him from finding room in us. The way of the Lord, as you have heard, is that he does all things within you, so that all our works are not ours but his, which comes by faith.

29. This, however, is not possible if you desire worthily to prepare yourself by praying, fasting, self-mortification, and your own works, as is now generally and foolishly taught during the time of Advent. A spiritual preparation is meant, consisting in a thoroughgoing knowledge and confession of your being unfit, a sinner, poor, damned, and miserable, with all the works you may perform. The more a heart is thus minded, the better it prepares the way of the Lord, although meanwhile possibly drinking fine wines, walking on roses, and not praying a word.

30. The hindrance, however, which obstructs the Lord's way, is formed not only in the coarse and palpable sin of adultery, wrath, haughtiness, avarice, etc., but rather in spiritual conceit and Pharisaical pride, which thinks highly of its own life and good works, feels secure, does not condemn itself, and would remain uncondemned by another.

Such, then, is the other class of men, namely, those that do not believe the crying of John, but call it the devil's, since it forbids good works and condemns the service of God, as they say. These are the people to whom most of all and most urgently it is said, "Prepare the way of the Lord," and who least of all accept it.

31. Therefore John speaks to them with cutting words in Luke 3:7–8, "Ye offspring of vipers, who warned you to flee from the wrath to come? Bring forth therefore fruits worthy of repentance." But, as said above, the more just people are urged to prepare the Lord's way, the more they obstruct it and the more unreasonable they become. They will not be told that their doings are not the Lord's, and finally, to the glory and honor of God, they annihilate the truth and the word of John, himself and his Master to boot.

32. Judge, then, whether it was not a mighty confession on the part of John, when he dared to open his mouth and proclaim that he was not Christ, but a voice to which they did not like to listen, chiding the great teachers and leaders of the people for not doing that which was right and the Lord's pleasure. And as it went with John, so it still goes, from the beginning of the world unto the end. For such conceited piety will not be told that it must first and foremost prepare the way of the Lord, imagining itself to sit in God's lap and desiring to be petted and flattered by having long ago finished the way, before God even thought of finding a way for them—those precious saints! The pope and his followers likewise have condemned the crying of John to prepare the Lord's way. Aye, it is an intolerable crying—except to poor, penitent sinners with aggrieved consciences, for whom it is the best of cordials.

33. But isn't it a perverse and strange manner of speaking to say, "I am the voice of one crying"? How can a man be a voice? He ought to have said, I

am one crying with a voice! But that it speaking according to the manner of the Scriptures. In Exodus 4:16, God spoke to Moses, "Aaron shall be to thee a mouth." And in Job 29:15, we read, "I was eyes to the blind, and feet was I to the lame." Similarly, we say of a man that gold is his heart and money his life.

So here, "I am the voice of one crying" means, I am one who cries, and have received my name from my office; even as Aaron is called a mouth because of his speaking, I am a voice because of my crying. And that which in Hebrew reads *vox clamantis*, the voice of one crying, would be translated into Latin *vox clamans*, a crying voice. Thus Saint Paul in Romans 15:26, says *pauperes sanctorum*, the poor of the saints, instead of *pauperes sancti*, the poor saints; and in 1 Timothy 3:16, *mysterium pietatis* (the mystery of godliness) instead of *mysterium pium* (the godly mystery). Instead of saying, The language of the Germans, I had better say, the German language. Thus "a voice of one crying" means "a crying voice." In Hebrew, there are many similar phrases.

> *And they had been sent from the Pharisees. And they asked him,*
> *and said unto him: "Why then baptizest thou if thou be not the Christ,*
> *nor Elijah, neither the prophet?" John answered them, saying, "I baptize*
> *with water; in the midst of you standeth one whom ye know not,*
> *even he that cometh after me is preferred before me,*
> *the latchet of whose shoes I am not worthy to unloose."*

34. It seems as though the evangelist had omitted something in these words, and as if John's complete answer ought to be, "I baptize with water; but he has come among you who baptizes with fire." Thus Luke, in Luke 3:16, says, "I baptize you with water: but he shall baptize you with fire." And, in Acts 1:5, we read, "John baptized with water, but ye shall be baptized with the Holy Ghost." But although he here says nothing of this other baptism, he sufficiently indicates that there is to be another baptism, since he speaks of another who is coming after him and who, undoubtedly, will not baptize with water.

35. Now begins the second onset, whereby John was tried on the other side. For not being able to move him by allurements, they attack him with threats. And here is uncovered their false humility, manifesting itself as pride and haughtiness. The same they would have done had John followed them, after they had had enough of him. Learn, therefore, here to be on your guard against men, particularly when they feign to be gentle and kind; as Christ says, in Matthew 10:16–17, "Beware of men, be wise as serpents, and harmless as doves." That is to say, Do not trust those that are smooth, and do no evil to your enemies.

36. Behold, these Pharisees, who professed their willingness to accept John as the Christ, veer around when things turn out as they desired, and censure John's baptism. They say, as it were, "Since you are not Christ, nor Elijah, nor a prophet, you are to know that we are your superiors according to the law of Moses, and you are, therefore, to conduct yourself as our subordinate. You are not to act independently, without our command, our knowledge, and without our permission. Who has given you power to introduce something new among our people with your baptizing? You are bringing yourself into trouble with your criminal disobedience."

37. John, however, as he had despised their hypocrisy, likewise scorns their threats, remains firm, and confesses Christ as before. Moreover, he boldly attacks them and charges them with ignorance, saying, as it were, "I have no authority from you to baptize with water. But what of that? There is another from whom I have power; him you do not know, but he is amply sufficient for me. If you knew him, or wished to know him, you would not ask whence I have power to baptize, but you would come to be baptized yourselves. For he is so much greater than I, that I am not worthy to unloose his shoes' latchet.

38. John's words, "He it is who, coming after me, is preferred before me," three times quoted by the evangelist in this chapter, have been misinterpreted and obscured by some who referred them to Christ's divine and eternal birth, as though John meant to say that Christ had been born before him in eternity. But what is remarkable is the fact that he was born before John in eternity, seeing that he was born before the world and all other things. Thus he was also to come not only after him, but after all things, since he is the first and the last, in Revelation 1:11. Therefore, his past and his future agree. John's words are clear and simple, referring to Christ when he already was a man. The words "He will come after me" cannot be taken to mean that he would be born after him; John, like Christ, was at that time about thirty years old.

39. These words then evidently apply to his preaching. He means to say, "I have come, that is, I have begun to preach, but I shall soon stop and another will come and preach after me." Thus Saint Luke says, in Acts 1:22, that Christ began from the baptism of John; and, in Luke 3:23, that Jesus was thirty years old when he began. And it says in Matthew 11:3, "Art thou he that should come," that is, he who should begin to preach; for Christ's office does not begin until after his baptism, at which his Father had acknowledged and glorified him. Then also began the New Testament and the time of grace, not at the birth of Christ, as he himself says, in Mark 1:15, "The time is fulfilled, and the kingdom of God is at hand." Had he not begun to preach, his birth would

have been of no use; but when he did begin to act and to teach, then were fulfilled all prophecies, all Scriptures; then came a new light and a new world.

40. So we see what he means by saying, "He will come after me." But the meaning of the words "He is preferred before me; he was before me" is not yet clear, some referring them to Christ's eternal birth. We maintain in all simplicity that those words also were spoken concerning their preaching. Thus the meaning is, "Although he is not yet preaching, but is coming after me, and I am preaching before him, nevertheless he is already at hand and so close by that, before I began to preach, he has already been there and has been appointed to preach. The words "before me," therefore, point to John's office and not to his person. Thus, "he has been before my preaching and baptism for about thirty years; but he has not yet come, and has not yet begun." John thereby indicates his office, namely, that he is not a prophet foretelling the coming of Christ, but one who precedes him who is already present, who is so near that he has already been in existence so many years before his beginning and coming.

41. Therefore, he also says, "In the midst of you standeth one whom ye know not." He means to say, "Do not permit your eyes to wander off into future ages. He of whom the prophets speak has been among you in the Jewish nation for well nigh thirty years. Take care and do not miss him. You do not know him, therefore, I have come to point him out to you." The words "In the midst of you standeth one" are spoken after the manner of the Scriptures, which say, A prophet will arise or stand up. Thus in Matthew 24:24, "There shall arise false prophets." In Deuteronomy 18:15, God says, "The Lord thy God will raise up unto thee a prophet." John now wishes to show that this "raising up, arising, standing," etc., was fulfilled in Christ, who was already standing among them, as God had prophesied; the people, however, knew him not.

42. This then is the other office of John and of every preacher of the Gospel, not alone to make all the world sinners, as we have heard above (§24ff.); but also to give comfort and show how we may get rid of our sins; this he does in pointing to him who is to come. Hereby he directs us to Christ, who is to redeem us from our sins, if we accept him in true faith. The first office says, "You are all sinners, and are wanting in the way of the Lord." When we believe this, the other office follows and says, "Listen, and accept Christ, believe in him; he will free you of your sins." If we believe this, we have it. Of this we shall say more anon.

These things were done in Bethany beyond the Jordan,
where John was baptizing.

43. So diligently does the evangelist record the testimony of John, that he also mentions the places where it happened. The confession of Christ is greatly dependent on testimony, and there are many difficulties in the way. Undoubtedly, however, he wished to allude to some spiritual mystery of which we shall now speak.

II. THE SPIRITUAL MEANING OF THIS GOSPEL STORY

44. This is the sum and substance of it: In this Gospel is pictured the preacher's office of the New Testament—what it is, what it does, and what happens to it.

45. First, it is the voice of one calling, not a piece of writing. The law and the Old Testament are dead writings, put into books, and the Gospel is to be a living voice. Therefore, John is an image, and a type, and also a pioneer, the first of all preachers of the Gospel. He writes nothing but calls out everything with his living voice.

46. Secondly, the Old Testament or the law was preached among the tents at Mount Sinai to the Jews alone. But John's voice is heard in the wilderness, freely and openly, under the heavens, before all the world.

47. Thirdly, it is a calling, clear and loud voice, that is to say, one that speaks boldly and undauntedly and fears no one, neither death, hell, life, nor the world, neither devil, man, honor, disgrace, nor any creature. Thus Isaiah says, in Isaiah 40:6ff., "The voice of one saying, cry. And one said, What shall I cry? All flesh is grass, and all the goodliness thereof is as the flower of the field. The grass withereth, the flower fadeth, but the Word of our God shall stand forever." And further, "O thou that tellest good tidings to Zion, get thee up on a high mountain; lift up thy voice with strength; lift it up, be not afraid." The world cannot bear the Gospel, and hence there must be a strength, which scorns it and can call against it without fear.

48. Fourthly, John's raiment is of camel's hair and has a leather girdle, in Matthew 3:4. This means the strict and chaste life of preachers, but above all it points to the manner of the preachers of the Gospel. It is a voice not given to soft phrases, neither does it deal in hypocrisy and flattery. It is a sermon of the cross, a hard, rough, sharp speech for the natural man, and girds the loins for spiritual and bodily chastity. This is taken from the life and words of the patriarchs of old, who like camels have borne the burden of the law and of the cross. "He eats locusts and wild honey." This means those that accept the Gospel, namely, the humble sinners, who take the Gospel unto and into themselves.

49. Fifthly, John is on the other side of the Jordan. "Jordan" really means the holy Scriptures, which have two sides. One, the left side, is the external

meaning which the Jews sought in Holy Writ; here John is not. For this interpretation does not produce sinners, but saints proud of their works. The right
side is the true spiritual understanding, which discards and kills all works, in
order that faith alone may remain, in all humility. This meaning is brought out
in the Gospels, as Saint Paul does, in Romans 3:23, saying, "All have sinned."

50. Sixthly, here begins the dispute between true and false preachers. The
Pharisees cannot bear to hear John's voice; they despise his teaching and baptism, and remain obdurate in their doings and teachings. On account of the
people, however, they pretend to think highly of him. But because he opposes
their will, he must be possessed of the devil, they say, and finally he must be
beheaded by Herod. So it is now and so it has always been. No false teacher
wishes it to be said of him that he preaches without or against the Gospel, but
on the contrary that he thinks highly of it and believes in it. Nevertheless he
does violence to it, making it conform to his meaning. This the Gospel cannot
permit, for it stands firm and never lies. Then it is reviled as heresy and error,
aye as a devilish doctrine, and finally they apply violence prohibiting it and
striking off its head so that it may nowhere be preached or heard. This was
done by the pope in the case of John Huss.

51. Thus he is a truly Christian preacher who preaches nothing but that
which John proclaimed, and firmly insists upon it.

First, he must preach the law so that the people may learn what great
things God demands of us; of these we cannot perform any because of the
impotence of our nature which has been corrupted by Adam's fall. Then
comes the baptism in Jordan. The cold water means the teaching of the law,
which does not kindle love but rather extinguishes it. For through the law man
learns how difficult and how impossible of fulfillment the law is. Then he
becomes hostile to it, and his love for it cools; he feels that he heartily hates it.
This of course is a grievous sin, to be hostile to God's commands. Therefore
man must humble himself, and confess that he is lost and that all his works are
sins, aye, that his whole life is sinful. Herewith then John's baptism has been
accomplished, and he has been not only besprinkled but properly baptized.
Then he sees why John says, "Repent ye." He understands that John is right,
and that everyone must needs become a better man and repent. But Pharisees
and those holy in their works do not arrive at this knowledge, nor do they
permit themselves to be baptized. They imagine that they do not need repentance and, therefore, John's words and baptism are foolishness in their eyes.

52. Furthermore, when the first teaching, that of the law, and baptism are
over and man, humiliated by the knowledge of himself, is forced to despair
of himself and his powers, then begins the second part of John's teaching,

in which he directs the people from himself to Christ and says, "Behold the Lamb of God that takes upon itself the sin of the world." By this he means to say, "First I have, by my teaching, made you all sinners, have condemned your works and told you to despair of yourselves. But in order that you may not also despair of God, behold, I will show you how to get rid of your sins and obtain salvation. Not that you can strip off your sins or make yourselves pious through your works; another man is needed for this; nor can I do it, I can point him out, however. It is Jesus Christ, the Lamb of God. He, he, and no one else either in heaven or on earth takes our sins upon himself. You yourself could not pay for the very smallest of sins. He alone must take upon himself not alone your sins, but the sins of the world, and not some sins, but all the sins of the world, be they great or small, many or few." This then is preaching and hearing the pure Gospel, and recognizing the finger of John, who points out to you Christ, the Lamb of God.

53. Now, if you are able to believe that this voice of John speaks the truth, and if you are able to follow his finger and recognize the Lamb of God carrying your sin, then you have gained the victory, then you are a Christian, a master of sin, death, hell, and all things. Then your conscience will rejoice and become heartily fond of this gentle Lamb of God. Then will you love, praise, and give thanks to our heavenly Father for this infinite wealth of his mercy, preached by John and given in Christ. And finally you will become cheerful and willing to do his divine will, as best you can, with all your strength. For what lovelier and more comforting message can be heard than that our sins are not ours any more, that they no more lie on us, but on the Lamb of God. How can sin condemn such an innocent Lamb? Lying on him, it must be vanquished and made to nothing, and likewise death and hell, being the reward of sin, must be vanquished also. Behold what God our Father has given us in Christ!

54. Take heed, therefore, take heed, I say, lest you presume to get rid of the smallest of your sins through your own merit before God, and lest you rob Christ, the Lamb of God, of his credit. John indeed demands that we grow better and repent; but that he does not mean us to grow better of ourselves and to strip off our sins by our own strength, this he declares powerfully by adding, "Behold the Lamb of God that taketh away the sin of the world." As we have said above (§29), he means that each one is to know himself and his need of becoming a better man; yet he is not to look for this in himself, but in Jesus Christ alone. Now may God our Father according to his infinite mercy bestow upon us this knowledge of Christ, and may he send into the world the voice of John, with great numbers of evangelists! Amen.

Christmas Day

❧❀❧

Of the Birth of Jesus, and of the Angels' Song of Praise at His Birth

Now it came to pass in those days, there went out a decree from Cæsar Augustus, that all the world should be enrolled. This was the first enrollment made when Quirinius was governor of Syria. And all went to enroll themselves, every one to his own city. And Joseph also went up from Galilee, out of the city of Nazareth, into Judea, to the city of David, which is called Bethlehem, because he was of the house and family of David; to enroll himself with Mary, who was betrothed to him, being great with child. And it came to pass, while they were there, the days were fulfilled that she should be delivered. And she brought forth her firstborn son; and she wrapped him in swaddling clothes, and laid him in a manger, because there was no room for them in the inn.

And there were shepherds in the same country abiding in the field, and keeping watch by night over their flock. And an angel of the Lord stood by them, and the glory of the Lord shone round about them; and they were sore afraid. And the angel said unto them, "Be not afraid; for behold, I bring you good tidings of great joy which shall be to all the people: for there is born to you this day in the city of David a Savior, who is Christ the Lord. And this is the sign unto you: Ye shall find a babe wrapped in swaddling clothes, and lying in a manger." And suddenly there was with the angel a multitude of the heavenly host praising God, and saying, "Glory to God in the highest, and on earth peace among men in whom he is well pleased." — LUKE 2:1–14

I. THE BIRTH OF JESUS

The Story of Jesus' Birth

1. It is written in Haggai 2:6–7, that God says, "I will shake the heavens; and the precious things of all nations shall come." This is fulfilled today, for the heavens were shaken, that is, the angels in the heavens sang praises to

God. And the earth was shaken, that is, the people on the earth were agitated;
one journeying to this city, another to that throughout the whole land, as the
Gospel tells us. It was not a violent, bloody uprising, but rather a peaceable
one awakened by God, who is the God of peace.

It is not to be understood that all countries upon earth were so agitated,
but only those under Roman rule, which did not comprise half of the whole
earth. However, no land was agitated as was the land of Judea, which had
been divided among the tribes of Israel, although at this time the land was
inhabited mostly by the race of Judah, as the ten tribes led captive into As-
syria never returned.

2. This taxing, enrollment, or census, says Luke, was the first; but in the
Gospel according to Matthew, in Matthew 17:24, and at other places, we read
that it was continued from time to time, that they even demanded tribute of
Christ, and tempted him with the tribute money, in Matthew 22:17. On the day
of his suffering, they also testified against him, that he forbade to give tribute
to Cæsar. The Jews did not like to pay tribute and unwillingly submitted to the
taxing, maintaining that they were God's people and free from Cæsar. They
had great disputes as to whether they were obliged to pay the tribute, but they
could not help themselves and were compelled to submit. For this reason, they
would have been pleased to draw Jesus into the discussion and bring him under
the Roman jurisdiction. This taxing was, therefore, nothing else but a common
decree throughout the whole empire that every individual should annually pay
a penny, and the officers who collected the tribute were called publicans, who
in German are improperly interpreted notorious sinners.

3. Observe how exact the evangelist is in his statement that the birth of
Christ occurred in the time of Cæsar Augustus, and when Quirinius was governor of Syria, of which the land of Judea was a part, just as Austria is a part of
the German land. This being the very first taxing, it appears that this tribute
was never before paid until just at the time when Christ was to be born. By
this, Jesus shows that his kingdom was not to be of an earthly character nor
to exercise worldly power and lordship, but that he, together with his parents,
is subject to the powers that be. Since he comes at the time of the very first
enrollment, he leaves no doubt with respect to this, for had he desired to
leave it in doubt, he might have willed to be born under another enrollment,
so that it might have been said it just happened so, without any divine intent.

4. And had he not willed to be submissive, he might have been born before there was any enrollment decreed. Since now all the works of Jesus are
precious teachings, this circumstance cannot be interpreted otherwise than
that he by divine counsel and purpose will not exercise any worldly authority,

but will be subject to it. This then is the first rebuke to the pope's government, and everything of that character, that harmonizes with the kingdom of Christ as night does with day.

5. This Gospel is so clear that it requires very little explanation, but it should be well considered and taken deeply to heart; and no one will receive more benefit from it than those who, with a calm, quiet heart, banish everything else from their mind and diligently look into it. It is just as the sun which is reflected in calm water and gives out vigorous warmth but which cannot be so readily seen nor can it give out such warmth in water that is in roaring and rapid motion.

Therefore, if you would be enlightened and warmed, if you would see the wonders of divine grace and have your heart aglow and enlightened, devout and joyful, go where you can silently meditate and lay hold of this picture deep in your heart, and you will see miracle upon miracle. But to give the common person a start and a motive to contemplate it, we will illustrate it in part and afterward enter into it more deeply.

6. First, behold how very ordinary and common things are to us that transpire on earth, and yet how high they are regarded in heaven. On earth it occurs in this wise: Here is a poor young woman, Mary of Nazareth, not highly esteemed, but of the humblest citizens of the village. No one is conscious of the great wonder she bears; she is silent, keeps her own counsel, and regards herself as the lowliest in the town. She starts out with her husband, Joseph; very likely, they had no servant, and he had to do the work of master and servant, and she that of mistress and maid. They were, therefore, obliged to leave their home unoccupied, or commend it to the care of others.

7. Now they evidently owned an ass, upon which Mary rode, although the Gospel does not mention it, and it is possible that she went on foot with Joseph. Imagine how she was despised at the inns and stopping places on the way, although worthy to ride in state in a chariot of gold.

There were, no doubt, many wives and daughters of prominent men at that time, who lived in fine apartments and great splendor, while the mother of God takes a journey in mid-winter under most trying circumstances. What distinctions there are in the world! It was more than a day's journey from Nazareth in Galilee to Bethlehem in the land of Judea. They had to journey either by or through Jerusalem, for Bethlehem is south of Jerusalem, while Nazareth is north.

8. The evangelist shows how, when they arrived at Bethlehem, they were the most insignificant and despised, so that they had to make way for others until they were obliged to take refuge in a stable, to share with the cattle,

lodging, table, bedchamber and bed, while many a wicked man sat at the head in the hotels and was honored as lord. No one noticed or was conscious of what God was doing in that stable. He lets the large houses and costly apartments remain empty, lets their inhabitants eat, drink, and be merry; but this comfort and treasure are hidden from them. O what a dark night this was for Bethlehem, that was not conscious of that glorious light! See how God shows that he utterly disregards what the world is, has, or desires; and furthermore, that the world shows how little it knows or notices what God is, has, and does.

9. See, this is the first picture with which Christ puts the world to shame and exposes all it does and knows. It shows that the world's greatest wisdom is foolishness, her best actions are wrong, and her greatest treasures are misfortunes. What had Bethlehem when it did not have Christ? What have they now who at that time had enough? What do Joseph and Mary lack now, although at that time they had no room to sleep comfortably?

10. Some have commented on the word *"diversorium,"* as if it meant an open archway, through which everybody could pass, where some asses stood, and that Mary could not get to a lodging place. This is not right. The evangelist desires to show that Joseph and Mary had to occupy a stable because there was no room for her in the inn, in the place where the pilgrim guests generally lodged. All the guests were cared for in the inn or caravansary, with room, food, and bed, except these poor people who had to creep into a stable where it was customary to house cattle.

This word *diversorium*, which by Luke is called *"katalyma,"* means nothing else than a place for guests, which is proved by the words of Christ, in Luke 22:11, where he sent the disciples to prepare the supper, "Go and say unto the master of the house, the Teacher saith unto thee, Where is the guest chamber, where I shall eat the Passover with my disciples?" So also here Joseph and Mary had no room in the *katalyma*, the inn, but only in the stable belonging to the innkeeper, who would not have been worthy to give shelter to such a guest. They had neither money nor influence to secure a room in the inn, hence they were obliged to lodge in a stable. O world, how stupid! O man, how blind thou art!

11. But the birth itself is still more pitiful. There was no one to take pity on this young wife who was for the first time to give birth to a child; no one to take to heart her condition that she, a stranger, did not have the least thing a mother needs in a birth night. There she is without any preparation, without either light or fire, alone in the darkness, without anyone's offering her service as is customary for women to do at such times. Everything is in commotion in the inn, there is a swarming of guests from all parts of the country, no one

thinks of this poor woman. It is also possible that she did not expect the event so soon, else she would probably have remained at Nazareth.

12. Just imagine what kind of swaddling clothes they were in which she wrapped the child. Possibly her veil or some article of her clothing she could spare. But that she should have wrapped him in Joseph's trousers, which are exhibited at Aix-la-Chapelle, appears entirely too false and frivolous. It is a fable, the like of which there are more in the world. Is it not strange that the birth of Christ occurs in cold winter, in a strange land, and in such a poor and despicable manner?

13. Some argue as to how this birth took place, as if Jesus was born while Mary was praying and rejoicing, without any pain, and before she was conscious of it. While I do not altogether discard that pious supposition, it was evidently invented for the sake of simple-minded people. But we must abide by the Gospel, that he was born of the Virgin Mary. There is no deception here, for the Word clearly states that it was an actual birth.

14. It is well known what is meant by giving birth. Mary's experience was not different from that of other women, so that the birth of Christ was a real natural birth, Mary being his natural mother and he being her natural son. Therefore, her body performed its functions of giving birth, which naturally belonged to it, except that she brought forth without sin, without shame, without pain, and without injury, just as she had conceived without sin. The curse of Eve did not come on her, where God said, "In pain thou shalt bring forth children," in Genesis 3:16; otherwise, it was with her in every particular as with every woman who gives birth to a child.

15. Grace does not interfere with nature and her work, but rather improves and promotes it. Likewise Mary, without doubt, also nourished the child with milk from her breast and not with strange milk, or in a manner different from that which nature provided, as we sing: *ubere de coelo pleno*, from her breast being filled by heaven, without injury or impurity. I mention this that we may be grounded in the faith and know that Jesus was a natural man in every respect just as we, the only difference being in his relation to sin and grace, he being without a sinful nature. In him and in his mother nature was pure in all the members and in all the operations of those members. No body or member of woman ever performed its natural function without sin, except that of this virgin; here for once God bestowed special honor upon nature and its operations. It is a great comfort to us that Jesus took upon himself our nature and flesh. Therefore, we are not to take away from him or his mother anything that is not in conflict with grace, for the text clearly says that she brought him forth, and the angels said, unto you he is born.

16. How could God have shown his goodness in a more sublime manner than by humbling himself to partake of flesh and blood, that he did not even disdain the natural privacy but honors nature most highly in that part where in Adam and Eve it was most miserably brought to shame? so that henceforth even that can be regarded godly, honest, and pure, which in all men is the most ungodly, shameful, and impure. These are real miracles of God, for in no way could he have given us stronger, more forcible, and purer pictures of chastity than in this birth. When we look at this birth, and reflect upon how the sublime Majesty moves with great earnestness and inexpressible love and goodness upon the flesh and blood of this virgin, we see how here all evil lust and every evil thought is banished.

17. No woman can inspire such pure thoughts in a man as this virgin; nor can any man inspire such pure thought in a woman as this child. If in reflecting on this birth we recognize the work of God that is embodied in it, only chastity and purity spring from it.

18. But what happens in heaven concerning this birth? As much as it is despised on earth, so much and a thousand times more is it honored in heaven. If an angel from heaven came and praised you and your work, would you not regard it of greater value than all the praise and honor the world could give you, and for which you would be willing to bear the greatest humility and reproach? What exalted honor is that when all the angels in heaven cannot restrain themselves from breaking out in rejoicing, so that even poor shepherds in the fields hear them preach, praise God, sing, and pour out their joy without measure? Were not all joy and honor realized at Bethlehem, yes, all joy and honor experienced by all the kings and nobles on earth, to be regarded as only dross and abomination, of which no one likes to think, when compared with the joy and glory here displayed?

19. Behold how very richly God honors those who are despised of men, and that very gladly. Here you see that his eyes look into the depths of humility, as is written, "He sitteth above the cherubim" and looketh into the depths. Nor could the angels find princes or valiant men to whom to communicate the good news; but only unlearned laymen, the most humble people upon earth. Could they not have addressed the high priests, who it was supposed knew so much concerning God and the angels? No, God chose poor shepherds, who, though they were of low esteem in the sight of men, were in heaven regarded as worthy of such great grace and honor.

20. See how utterly God overthrows that which is lofty! And yet we rage and rant for nothing but this empty honor, as we had no honor to seek in

heaven; we continually step out of God's sight so that he may not see us in the depths into which he alone looks.

21. This has been considered sufficiently for plain people. Everyone should ponder it further for himself. If every word is properly grasped, it is as fire that sets the heart aglow, as God says in Jeremiah 23:29, "Is not my Word like fire?" And as we see, it is the purpose of the divine Word to teach us to know God and his work, and to see that this life is nothing. For as he does not live according to this life and does not have possessions nor temporal honor and power, he does not regard these and says nothing concerning them, but teaches only the contrary. He works in opposition to these temporal things, looks with favor upon that from which the world turns, teaches that from which it flees, and takes up that which it discards.

22. And although we are not willing to tolerate such acts of God and do not want to receive blessing, honor, and life in this way, yet it must remain so. God does not change his purpose, nor does he teach or act differently than he purposed. We must adapt ourselves to him; he will not adapt himself to us. Moreover, he who will not regard his word, nor the manner in which he works to bring comfort to men, has assuredly no good evidence of being saved. In what more lovely manner could he have shown his grace to the humble and despised of earth than through this birth in poverty, over which the angels rejoice, and make it known to no one but to the poor shepherds?

23. Let us now look at the mysteries set before us in this history. In all the mysteries here, two things are especially set forth, the Gospel and faith, that is, what is to be preached and what is to be believed, who are to be the preachers and who are to be the believers. This we will now consider.

II. THE BIRTH OF JESUS CONSIDERED IN ITS SPIRITUAL MEANING

A. The Teaching Concerning Faith

24. Faith is first, and it is right that we recognize it as the most important in every word of God. It is of no value only to believe that this history is true as it is written; for all sinners, even those condemned believe that. The Scripture, God's Word, does not teach concerning faith that it is a natural work, without grace. The right and gracious faith which God demands is that you firmly believe that Christ is born for you, and that this birth took place for your welfare. The Gospel teaches that Christ was born, and that he did and suffered everything in our behalf, as is here declared by the angel, "Behold, I

bring you good tidings of great joy which shall be to all the people; for there is born to you this day a Savior, who is Christ the Lord." In these words, you clearly see that he is born for us.

25. He does not simply say, Christ is born, but to you he is born; neither does he say, I bring glad tidings, but to you I bring glad tidings of great joy. Furthermore, this joy was not to remain in Christ, but it shall be to all the people. This faith no condemned or wicked man has, nor can he have it; for the right ground of salvation which unites Christ and the believing heart is that they have all things in common. But what have they?

26. Christ has a pure, innocent, and holy birth. Man has an unclean, sinful, condemned birth; as David says, in Psalm 51:5, "Behold I was brought forth in iniquity; and in sin did my mother conceive me." Nothing can help this unholy birth except the pure birth of Christ. But Christ's birth cannot be distributed in a material sense neither would that avail anything; it is, therefore, imparted spiritually, through the Word; as the angel says, it is given to all who firmly believe so that no harm will come to them because of their impure birth. This it the way and manner in which we are to be cleansed from the miserable birth we have from Adam. For this purpose, Christ willed to be born, that through him we might be born again, as he says, in John 3:3, that it takes place through faith; as also Saint James says in James 1:18: "Of his own will he brought us forth by the word of truth, that we should be a kind of first-fruits of his creatures."

27. We see here how Christ, as it were, takes our birth from us and absorbs it in his birth, and grants us his, that in it we might become pure and holy, as if it were our own, so that every Christian may rejoice and glory in Christ's birth as much as if he had himself been born of Mary as was Christ. Whoever does not believe this, or doubts, is no Christian.

28. O, this is the great joy of which the angel speaks. This is the comfort and exceeding goodness of God that, if a man believes this, he can boast of the treasure that Mary is his rightful mother, Christ his brother, and God his father. For these things actually occurred and are true, but we must believe. This is the principal thing and the principal treasure in every Gospel, before any doctrine of good works can be taken out of it. Christ must above all things become our own and we become his, before we can do good works.

But this cannot occur except through the faith that teaches us rightly to understand the Gospel and properly to lay hold of it. This is the only way in which Christ can be rightly known so that the conscience is satisfied and made to rejoice. Out of this grow love and praise to God, who in Christ has bestowed upon us such unspeakable gifts. This gives courage to do or leave undone, and living or dying, to suffer everything that is well pleasing to God. This is what is meant by Isaiah 9:6, "Unto us a child is born, unto us a son is given," to us, to us, to us is born, and to us is given this child.

29. Therefore, see to it that you do not find pleasure in the Gospel only as a history, for that is only transcient; neither regard it only as an example, for it is of no value without faith; but see to it that you make this birth your own and that Christ be born in you. This will be the case if you believe, then you will repose in the lap of the Virgin Mary and be her dear child. But you must exercise this faith and pray while you live; you cannot establish it too firmly. This is our foundation and inheritance, upon which good works must be built.

30. If Christ has now thus become your own, and you have by such faith been cleansed through him and have received your inheritance without any personal merit, but alone through the love of God who gives to you as your own the treasure and work of his Son, it follows that you will do good works by doing to your neighbor as Christ has done to you. Here good works are their own teacher. What are the good works of Christ? Is it not true that they are good because they have been done for your benefit, for God's sake, who commanded him to do the works in your behalf? In this then Christ was obedient to the Father, in that he loved and served us.

31. Therefore since you have received enough and become rich, you have no other commandment to serve Christ and render obedience to him, than so to direct your works that they may be of benefit to your neighbor, just as the works of Christ are of benefit and use to you. For the reason Jesus said at the Last Supper, "This is my commandment that ye love one another; even as I have loved you," in John 13:34. Here it is seen that he loved us and did everything for our benefit, in order that we may do the same, not to him, for he needs it not, but to our neighbor; this is his commandment, and this is our obedience. Therefore, it is through faith that Christ becomes our own, and his love is the cause that we are his. He loves, we believe, thus both are united into one. Again, our neighbor believes and expects our love; we are, therefore, to love him also in return and not let him long for it in vain. One is the same as the other; as Christ helps us so we in return help our neighbor, and all have enough.

32. Observe now from this how far those have gone out of the way who have united good works with stone, wood, clothing, eating, and drinking. Of what benefit is it to your neighbor if you build a church entirely out of gold? Of what benefit to him is the frequent ringing of great church bells? Of what benefit to him is the glitter and the ceremonies in the churches, the priests' gowns, the sanctuary, the silver pictures and vessels? Of what benefit to him

are the many candles and much incense? Of what benefit to him is the much chanting and mumbling, the singing of vigils and masses? Do you think that God will permit himself to be paid with the sound of bells, the smoke of candles, the glitter of gold, and such fancies? He has commanded none of these. But if you see your neighbor going astray, sinning, or suffering in body or soul, you are to leave everything else and at once help him in every way in your power and, if you can do no more, help him with words of comfort and prayer. Thus has Christ done to you and given you an example for you to follow.

33. These are the two things in which a Christian is to exercise himself, the one that he draws Christ into himself, and that by faith he makes him his own, appropriates to himself the treasures of Christ, and confidently builds upon them; the other that he condescends to his neighbor and lets him share in that which he has received, even as he shares in the treasures of Christ. He who does not exercise himself in these two things will receive no benefit even if he should fast unto death, suffer torture, or even give his body to be burned, and were able to do all miracles, as Saint Paul teaches, in 1 Corinthians 13ff.

B. The Spiritual Meaning of the Doctrine of This Gospel

34. The other mystery, or spiritual teaching, is, that in the churches the Gospel only should be preached and nothing more. Now it is evident that the Gospel teaches nothing but the foregoing two things, Christ and his example and two kinds of good works, the one belonging to Christ by which we are saved through faith, the other belonging to us by which our neighbor receives help. Whosoever therefore teaches anything different from the Gospel leads people astray; and whosoever does not teach the Gospel in these two parts leads people all the more astray and is worse than the former, who teaches without the Gospel, because he abuses and corrupts God's Word, as Saint Paul complains concerning some, in 2 Corinthians 2:17.

35. Now it is clear that nature could not have discovered such a doctrine, nor could all the ingenuity, reason, and wisdom of the world have thought it out. Who would be able to discover by means of his own efforts, that faith in Christ makes us one with Christ and gives us for our own all that is Christ's? Who would be able to discover that no works are of any value except those intended to benefit our neighbor? Nature teaches no more than that which is wrought by the law. Therefore it falls back upon its own work, so that this one thinks he fulfills the commandment by founding some institution or order, that one by fasting, this one by the kind of clothes he wears, that one by going on pilgrimages; this one in this manner, that one in that manner;

and yet all their works are worthless, for no one is helped by them. Such is the case at the present time in which the whole world is blinded and is going astray through the doctrines and works of men, so that faith and love along with the Gospel have perished.

36. Therefore, the Gospel properly apprehended is a supernatural sermon and light that makes known Christ only. This is pointed out first of all by the fact that it was not a man that made it known to others, but that an angel came down from heaven and made known to the shepherds the birth of Jesus, while no human being knew anything about it.

37. In the second place, it is pointed out by the fact that Christ was born at midnight, by which he indicates that all the world is in darkness as to its future and that Christ cannot be known by mere reason, but that knowledge concerning him must be revealed from heaven.

38. In the third place, it is shown by the light that shined around the shepherds, which teaches that here there must be an entirely different light than that of human reason. Moreover, when Saint Luke says, *Gloria Dei*, the glory of God, shone around them, he calls that light a brightness, or the glory of God. Why does he say that? In order to call attention to the mystery and reveal the character of the Gospel. For while the Gospel is a heavenly light that teaches nothing more than Christ, in whom God's grace is given to us and all human merit is entirely cast aside, it exalts only the glory of God, so that henceforth no one may be able to boast of his own power, but must give God the glory, that it is of his love and goodness alone that we are saved through Christ.

See, the divine honor, the divine glory, is the light in the Gospel, which shines around us from heaven through the apostles and their followers who preach the Gospel. The angel here was in the place of all the preachers of the Gospel, and the shepherds in the place of all the hearers, as we shall see. For this reason, the Gospel can tolerate no other teaching besides its own; for the teaching of men is earthly light and human glory; it exalts the honor and praise of men, and makes souls to glory in their own works, while the Gospel glories in Christ, in God's grace and goodness, and teaches us to boast of and confide in Christ.

39. In the fourth place, this is represented by the name Judea and Bethlehem, where Christ chose to be born. Judea is interpreted, confession or thanksgiving; as when we confess, praise, and thank God, acknowledging that all we possess are his gifts. One who so confesses and praises is called *Judaeus*. Such a king of the Jews is Christ, as the expression is, "*Jesus Nazarenus Rex Judaeorum*," Jesus the Nazarene, the king of the Jews, of those confessing

God. By this is shown that no teaching whatever can make such a confession except the Gospel, which teaches Christ.

40. Beth means house; *lehem* means bread—Bethlehem, a house of bread. The city had that name because it was situated in a good, fruitful country, rich in grain, so that it was the granary for the neighboring towns or, as we would call it, a fertile country. In olden times, the name of the city was Ephrata, which means fruitful. Both names imply that the city was in a fruitful and rich land. By this is represented that without the Gospel this earth is a wilderness and there is no confession of God nor thanksgiving.

41. Moreover, where Christ and the Gospel are, there is the fruitful Bethlehem and the thankful Judea. There everyone has enough in Christ and overflows with thanksgiving for the divine grace. But while men are thankful for human teachings, they cannot satisfy, but leave a barren land and deadly hunger. No heart can ever be satisfied unless it hears Christ rightly proclaimed in the Gospel. In this, a man comes to Bethlehem and finds him; he also comes to and remains in Judea and thanks his God eternally. Here he is satisfied; here God receives his praise and confession, while outside of the Gospel there is nothing but thanklessness and starvation.

42. But the angel shows most clearly that nothing is to be preached in Christendom except the Gospel; he takes upon himself the office of a preacher of the Gospel. He does not say, I preach to you, but "glad tidings I bring to you." I am an evangelist and my word is an evangel, good news. The meaning of the word Gospel is, a good, joyful message, that is preached in the New Testament. Of what does the Gospel testify? Listen! the angel says, "I bring you glad tidings of great joy," my Gospel speaks of great joy. Where is it? Hear again, "For there is born to you this day in the city of David a Savior, who is Christ the Lord."

43. Behold here what the Gospel is, namely, a joyful sermon concerning Christ, our Savior. Whoever preaches him rightly, preaches the Gospel of pure joy. How is it possible for man to hear of greater joy than that Christ has given to him as his own? He does not only say Christ is born, but he makes his birth our own by saying, to you a Savior.

44. Therefore the Gospel does not only teach the history concerning Christ, but it enables all who believe it to receive it as their own, which is the way the Gospel operates, as has just been set forth. Of what benefit would it be to me if Christ had been born a thousand times, and it would daily be sung into my ears in a most lovely manner, if I were never to hear that he was born for me and was to be my very own? If the voice gives forth this pleasant sound, even if it be in homely phrase, my heart listens with joy for it is a

lovely sound which penetrates the soul. If now there were anything else to be preached, the evangelical angel and the angelic evangelist would certainly have touched upon it.

C. The Spiritual Meaning of the Signs, the Angel, and the Shepherds

45. The angel says further, "And this is the sign unto you; Ye shall find the babe wrapped in swaddling clothes, and lying in a manger." The clothes are nothing else than the holy Scriptures, in which the Christian truth lies wrapped, in which the faith is described. For the Old Testament contains nothing else than Christ as he is preached in the Gospel. Therefore, we see how the apostles appeal to the testimony of the Scriptures and with them prove everything that is to be preached and believed concerning Christ. Thus Saint Paul says, in Romans 3:21, that the faith of Christ through which we become righteous is witnessed by the law and the prophets. And Christ himself, after his resurrection, opened to them the Scriptures, which speak of him, in Luke 24:27.

When he was transfigured on the mount, in Matthew 17:3, Moses and Elijah stood by him; that means, the law and the prophets as his two witnesses, which are signs pointing to him. Therefore, the angel says, the sign by which he is recognized is the swaddling clothes, for there is no other testimony on earth concerning Christian truth than the holy Scriptures.

46. According to this, Christ's seamless coat which was not divided and which during his sufferings was gambled off and given away, in John 19:23–24, represents the New Testament. It indicates that the pope, the Antichrist, would not deny the Gospel, but would shut it up violently and play with it by means of false interpretation until Christ is no longer to be found in it. Then the four soldiers who crucified the Lord are figures of all the bishops and teachers in the four quarters of the earth, who violently suppress the Gospel and destroy Christ and his faith by means of their human teachings, as the pope with his papists has long since done.

47. From this, we see that the law and the prophets cannot be rightly preached and known unless we see Christ wrapped up in them. It is true that Christ does not seem to be in them, nor do the Jews find him there. They appear to be insignificant and unimportant clothes, simple words, which seem to speak of unimportant external matters, the import of which is not recognized; but the New Testament, the Gospel, must open it, throw its light upon it, and reveal it, as has been said.

48. First of all, then, the Gospel must be heard, and the appearance and the voice of the angel must be believed. Had the shepherds not heard from

the angel that Christ lay there, they might have seen him ten thousand times without ever knowing that the child was Christ. Accordingly, Saint Paul says, in 2 Corinthians 3:16, that the law remains dark and covered up for the Jews until they are converted to Christ.

Christ must first be heard in the Gospel, then it will be seen how beautiful and lovely the whole Old Testament is in harmony with him, so that a man cannot help giving himself in submission to faith and be enabled to recognize the truth of what Christ says in John 5:46, "For if ye believed Moses, ye would believe me, for he wrote of me."

49. Therefore, let us beware of all teaching that does not set forth Christ. What more would you know? What more do you need if indeed you know Christ, as above set forth, if you walk by faith in God, and by love to your neighbor, doing to your fellow man as Christ has done to you. This is indeed the whole Scripture in its briefest form, that no more words or books are necessary, but only life and action.

50. He lies in the manger. Notice here that nothing but Christ is to be preached throughout the whole world. What is the manger but the congregations of Christians in the churches to hear the preaching? We are the beasts before this manger; and Christ is laid before us upon whom we are to feed our souls. Whosoever goes to hear the preaching, goes to this manger; but it must be the preaching of Christ. Not all mangers have Christ, neither do all sermons teach the true faith. There was but one manger in Bethlehem in which this treasure lay and, besides, it was an empty and despised manger in which there was no fodder.

Therefore, the preaching of the Gospel is divorced from all other things; it has and teaches nothing besides Christ. Should anything else be taught, then it is no more the manger of Christ, but the manger of warhorses full of temporal things and of fodder for the body.

51. But in order to show that Christ in swaddling clothes represents the faith in the Old Testament, we will here give several examples. We read, in Matthew 8:4, when Christ cleansed the leper, that he said to him, "Go, show thyself to the priest, and offer the gift that Moses commanded, for a testimony unto them." Here you perceive that the law of Moses was given to the Jews for a testimony, or sign, as the angel also here says, namely, that such law represents something different from itself. What? Christ is the priest, all men are spiritual lepers because of unbelief; but when we come to faith in him, he touches us with his hand, gives and lays upon us his merit, and we become clean and whole without any merit on our part whatever. We are, therefore, to show our gratitude to him and acknowledge that we have not become

pious by our own works but through his grace; then our course will be right before God. In addition, we are to offer our gifts, that is, give of our own to help our fellow man, to do good to him as Christ has done to us. Thus Christ is served and an offering is brought to the rightful priest, for it is done for his sake, in order to love and praise him.

Do you here see how, figuratively speaking, Christ and the faith are wrapped up in the plain Scriptures? It is here made evident how Moses in the law gave only testimony and an interpretation of Christ. The whole Old Testament should be understood in this manner, and should be taken to be the swaddling clothes as a sign pointing out and making Christ known.

52. Again, it was commanded that the Sabbath should be strictly observed and no work should be done, which shows that not our works but Christ's works should dwell in us; for it is written that we are not saved by our works but by the works of Christ. Now these works of Christ are twofold, as shown before—on the one hand, those that Christ has done personally without us, which are the most important and in which we believe; the others, those he performs in us, in our love to our neighbor. The first may be called the evening works and the second the morning works, so that evening and morning make one day, as it is written in Genesis 1:5, for the Scriptures begin the day in the evening and end in the morning, that is, the evening with the night is the first half, the morning with the day is the second half of the whole natural day. Now as the first half is dark and the second half is light, so the first works of Christ are concealed in our faith, but the others, the works of love, are to appear, to be openly shown toward our fellow man. Here then you see how the whole Sabbath is observed and hallowed.

53. Do you see how beautifully Christ lies in these swaddling clothes? How beautifully the Old Testament reveals the faith and love of Christ and of his Christians? Now, swaddling clothes are as a rule of two kinds, the outside of coarse woolen cloth, the inner of linen. The outer or coarse woolen cloth represents the testimony of the law, but the linen are the words of the prophets. As Isaiah says, in Isaiah 7:14, "Behold, a virgin shall conceive, and bear a son, and shall call his name Immanuel," and similar passages that would not be understood of Christ, had the Gospel not revealed it and shown that Christ is in them.

54. Here then we have these two, the faith and the Gospel, that these and nothing else are to be preached throughout Christendom. Let us now see who are to be the preachers and who the learners. The preachers are to be angels, that is, God's messengers, who are to lead a heavenly life, are to be constantly engaged with God's Word that they, under no circumstances,

preach the doctrine of men. It is a most incongruous thing to be God's messenger and not to further God's message. Angelus means a messenger, and Luke calls him God's messenger (*Angelus Domini*). The message also is of more importance than the messenger's life. If he leads a wicked life, he injures only himself, but if he brings a false message in the place of God's message, he leads astray and injures everyone that hears him, and causes idolatry among the people in that they accept lies for the truth, honor men instead of God, and pray to the devil instead of to God.

55. There is no more terrible plague, misfortune, or cause for distress upon earth than a preacher who does not preach God's Word, of whom, alas, the world today is full; and yet they think they are pious and do good when indeed their whole work is nothing but murdering souls, blaspheming God, and setting up idolatry, so that it would be much better for them if they were robbers, murderers, and the worst scoundrels, for then they would know that they are doing wickedly. But now they go along under spiritual names and show, as priest, bishop, pope, and are at the same time ravening wolves in sheep's clothing, and it would be well if no one ever heard their preaching.

56. The learners are shepherds, poor people out in the fields. Here Jesus does what he says, in Matthew 11:5, "And the poor have good tidings preached to them," and, in Matthew 5:3, "Blessed are the poor in spirit; for theirs is the kingdom of heaven." Here are no learned, no rich, no mighty ones, for such people do not as a rule accept the Gospel. The Gospel is a heavenly treasure, which will not tolerate any other treasure, and will not agree with any earthly guest in the heart. Therefore, whoever loves the one must let go the other, as Christ says, in Matthew 6:24, "You cannot serve God and mammon."

This is shown by the shepherds in that they were in the field, under the canopy of heaven, and not in houses, showing that they do not hold fast and cling to temporal things; and, besides, they are in the fields by night, despised by and unknown to the world, which sleeps in the night, and by day delights so to walk that it may be noticed; but the poor shepherds go about their work at night. They represent all the lowly who live on earth, often despised and unnoticed but dwell only under the protection of heaven. They eagerly desire the Gospel.

57. That there were shepherds, means that no one is to hear the Gospel for himself alone, but everyone is to tell it to others who are not acquainted with it. For he who believes for himself has enough and should endeavor to bring others to such faith and knowledge, so that one may be a shepherd of the other, to wait upon and lead him into the pasture of the Gospel in this world, during the nighttime of this earthly life.

At first, the shepherds were sore afraid because of the angel; for human nature is shocked when it first hears in the Gospel that all our works are nothing and are condemned before God, for it does not easily give up its prejudices and presumptions.

58. Now let everyone examine himself in the light of the Gospel and see how far he is from Christ, what is the character of his faith and love. There are many who are enkindled with dreamy devotion and, when they hear of such poverty of Christ, are almost angry with the citizens of Bethlehem, denounce their blindness and ingratitude, and think, if they had been there, they would have shown the Lord and his mother a more becoming service, and would not have permitted them to be treated so miserably. But they do not look by their side to see how many of their fellow men need their help, and which they let go on in their misery unaided. Who is there upon earth that has no poor, miserable, sick, erring ones, or sinful people around him? Why does he not exercise his love to those? Why does he not do to them as Christ has done to him?

59. It is altogether false to think that you have done much for Christ if you do nothing for those needy ones. Had you been at Bethlehem, you would have paid as little attention to Christ as they did; but since it is now made known who Christ is, you profess to serve him. Should he come now and lay himself in a manger, and would send you word that it was he, of whom you now know so much, you might do something for him, but you would not have done it before. Had it been positively made known to the rich man in the Gospel, to what high position Lazarus would be exalted, and he would have been convinced of the fact, he would not have left him lie and perish as he did.

60. Therefore, if your neighbor were now what he shall be in the future, and lay before you, you would surely give him attention. But now, since it is not so, you beat the air and do not recognize the Lord in your neighbor; you do not do to him as he has done to you. Therefore, God permits you to be blinded, and deceived by the pope and false preachers, so that you squander on wood, stone, paper, and wax that with which you might help your fellow man.

III. EXPLANATION OF THE ANGELS' SONG OF PRAISE

61. Finally, we must also treat of the angels' song, which we use daily in our service: *Gloria in Excelsis Deo*. There are three things to be considered in this song, the glory to God, the peace to the earth, and the good will to mankind. The good will might be understood as the divine good will God

has toward men through Christ. But we will admit it to mean the good will that is granted unto men through this birth, as it is set forth in the words thus, *"en anthropis eudokia, hominibus beneplacitum."*

62. The first is the glory to God. Thus we should also begin, so that in all things the praise and glory be given to God as the one who does, gives, and possesses all things, that no one ascribe anything to himself or claim any merit for himself. For the glory belongs to no one but to God alone; it does not permit of being made common by being shared by any person.

63. Adam stole the glory through the evil spirit and appropriated it to himself, so that all men with him have come into disgrace, which evil is so deeply rooted in all mankind that there is no vice in them as great as vanity. Everyone is well pleased with himself, and no one wants to be nothing, and they desire nothing, which spirit of vanity is the cause of all distress, strife, and war upon earth.

64. Christ has again brought back the glory to God, in that he has taught us how all we have or can do is nothing but wrath and displeasure before God, so that we may not be boastful and self-satisfied, but rather be filled with fear and shame, so that in this manner our glory and self-satisfaction may be crushed, and we be glad to be rid of it, in order that we may be found and preserved in Christ.

65. The second is the peace on earth. For just as strife must exist where God's glory is not found, as Solomon says, in Proverbs 13:10, "By pride cometh only contention"; so also, where God's glory is, there must be peace. Why should they quarrel when they know that nothing is their own, but that all they are, have, and can desire is from God; they leave everything in his hands and are content that they have such a gracious God. He knows that all he may have is nothing before God; he does not seek his own honor, but thinks of him who is something before God, namely, Christ.

66. From this, it follows that where there are true Christians, there is no strife, contention, or discord; as Isaiah says, in Isaiah 2:4, "And they shall beat their swords into plowshares, and their spears into pruning hooks; nation shall not lift up sword against nation, neither shall they learn war any more!"

67. Therefore, our Lord Christ is called a king of peace and is represented by King Solomon, whose name implies rich in peace, that inwardly he may give us peace in our conscience toward God through faith and, outwardly, that we may exercise love to our fellow men, so that through him there may be everywhere peace on earth.

68. The third is good will toward men. By good will is not meant the will that does good works, but the good will and peace of heart, which is equally

submissive in everything that may betide, be it good or evil. The angels knew very well that the peace, of which they sang, does not extend farther than to the Christians who truly believe; such have certainly peace among themselves. But the world and the devil have no reproof; they do not permit them to have peace but persecute them to death, as Christ says, in John 16:33, "In me ye may have peace. In the world ye have tribulation."

69. Hence it was not enough for the angels to sing peace on earth; they added to it the good will toward men, that they take pleasure in all that God does, regard all God's dealing with them as wise and good, and praise and thank him for it. They do not murmur but willingly submit to God's will. Moreover, since they know that God, whom they have received by faith in Christ as a gracious Father, can do all things, they exult and rejoice even under persecution, as Saint Paul says in Romans 5:3, "We also rejoice in our tribulations." They regard all that happens to them as for the best, out of the abundant satisfaction they have in Christ.

70. Behold, it is such a good will, pleasure, good opinion in all things, whether good or evil, that the angels wish to express in their song; for where there is no good will, peace will not long exist. The unbelieving put the worst construction on everything, always magnify the evil, and double every mishap. Therefore, God's dealings with them does not please them; they would have it different, and that which is written in Psalm 18:25–26, is fulfilled: "With the merciful thou wilt show thyself merciful, with the perfect man thou wilt show thyself perfect; with the pure thou wilt show thyself pure," that is, whoever has such pleasure in all things that you do in him, you, and all yours, will also have pleasure, and, "with the perverse thou wilt show thyself forward," that is, as you and all you do, does not please him, so he is not well pleasing to you and all that are yours.

71. Concerning the good will, Saint Paul says, in 1 Corinthians 10:33, "Even as I also please all men in all things." How does he do that? If you are content and satisfied with everything, you will in turn please everybody. It is a short rule: if you will please no one, be pleased with no one; if you will please everyone, be pleased with everyone—insofar, however, that you do not violate God's Word for, in that case, all pleasing and displeasing ceases. But what may be omitted without doing violence to God's Word, may be omitted, that you may please everyone and at the same time be faithful to God, then you have this good will of which the angels sing.

72. From this song, we may learn what kind of creatures the angels are. Don't consider what the great masters of art dream about them; here they are all painted in such a manner that their heart and their own thoughts may

be recognized. In the first place, in that they joyfully sing, ascribing the glory to God, they show how full of his light and fire they are, not praising themselves, but recognizing that all things belong to God alone, so that with great earnestness they ascribe the glory to him to whom it belongs. Therefore, if you would think of a humble, pure, obedient, and joyful heart, praising God, think of the angels. This is their first step, that by which they serve God.

73. The second is their love to us as has been shown. Here you see what great and gracious friends we have in them, that they favor us no less than themselves; rejoice in our welfare quite as much as they do in their own, so much so that in this song they give us a most comforting inducement to regard them as the best of friends. In this way, you rightly understand the angels, not according to their being, which the masters of art attempt fearlessly to portray, but according to their inner heart, spirit, and sense, that though I know not what they are, I know what their chief desire and constant work is; by this you look into their heart. This is enough concerning this Gospel. What is meant by Mary, Joseph, Nazareth will be explained in Luke 1.

The Armor of This Gospel

74. In this Gospel is the foundation of the article of our faith when we say, "I believe in Jesus Christ, born of the Virgin Mary." Although the same article is founded on different passages of Scripture, yet on none so clearly as on this one. Saint Mark says no more than that Christ has a mother; the same is also the case with Saint John, neither saying anything of his birth. Saint Matthew says he is born of Mary in Bethlehem, but lets it remain at that without gloriously proclaiming the virginity of Mary, as we will hear in due time. But Luke describes it clearly and diligently.

75. In olden times, it was also proclaimed by patriarchs and prophets; as when God says to Abraham, in Genesis 22:17, "And in thy seed shall all the nations of the earth be blessed." Again he says to David, in Psalm 89:4 and Psalm 132:11, "Jehovah hath sworn unto David in truth; he will not return from it; of the fruit of thy body will I set upon thy throne." But those are obscure words compared with the Gospel.

76. Again, it is also represented in many figures, as in the rod of Aaron which budded in a supernatural manner, although a dry piece of wood, in Numbers 7:5. So also Mary, exempt from all natural generation, brought forth, in a supernatural manner, really and truly a natural son, just as the rod bore natural almonds, and still remained a natural rod. Again by Gideon's fleece, in Judges 6:37, which was wet by the dew of heaven, while the land around it remained dry, and many like figures which it is not necessary to enumerate.

Nor do these figures conflict with faith, they rather adorn it; for it must at first be firmly believed before I can believe that the figure serves to illustrate it.

77. There is a great deal in this article, of which, in time of temptation, we would not be deprived, for the evil spirit attacks nothing so severely as our faith. Therefore, it is of the greatest importance for us to know where in God's Word this faith is set forth and, in time of temptation, point to that, for the evil spirit cannot stand against God's Word.

78. There are also many ethical teachings in the Gospel, as for example, meekness, patience, poverty, and the like; but these are touched upon enough and are not points of controversy, for they are fruits of faith and good works.

Christmas Day

❧✲❧

Christ's Titles of Honor and Attribute; Christ's Coming; His Becoming Man; and the Revelation of His Glory

*I*n the beginning was the Word, and the Word was with God, and the Word was God. The same was in the beginning with God. All things were made through him; and without him was not anything made that hath been made. In him was life; and the life was the light of men. And the light shineth in the darkness; and the darkness apprehended it not. There came a man, sent from God, whose name was John. The same came for witness, that he might bear witness of the light, that all might believe through him. He was not the light, but came that he might bear witness of the light. There was the true light, even the light which lighteth every man, coming into the world. He was in the world, and the world was made through him, and the world knew him not. He came unto his own, and they that were his own received him not. But as many as received him, to them gave he the right to become children of God, even to them that believe on his name: who were born, not of blood, nor of the will of the flesh, nor of the will of man, but of God. And the Word became flesh, and dwelt among us (and) we beheld his glory, glory as of the only begotten from the Father, full of grace and truth.* — JOHN 1:1–14

CHRIST'S TITLES OF HONOR AND ATTRIBUTE

1. This is the most important of all the Gospels of the church year, and yet it is not, as some think, obscure or difficult. For upon it is clearly founded the important article of faith concerning the divinity of Christ, with which all Christians ought to be acquainted, and which they are able to understand. Nothing is too great for faith. Therefore, let us consider this Gospel lesson in the simplest manner possible, and not as the Scholastics did with their fabricated subtleties, conceal its doctrine from the common people and frighten them away from it. There is no need of many fine and sharp distinctions, but only of a plain, simple explanation of the words of the text.

2. In the first place, we should know that all that the apostles taught and wrote, they took out of the Old Testament; for in it all things are proclaimed that were to be fulfilled later in Christ, and were to be preached, as Paul says in Romans 1:2, "God promised afore the Gospel of his son Jesus Christ through his prophets in the holy Scriptures." Therefore, all their preaching is based upon the Old Testament, and there is not a word in the New Testament that does not look back into the Old, where it had been foretold.

Thus we have seen in the Epistle how the divinity of Christ is confirmed by the apostle from passages in the Old Testament. For the New Testament is nothing more than a revelation of the Old. Just as one receives a sealed letter which is not to be opened until after the writer's death, so the Old Testament is the will and testament of Christ, which he has had opened after his death and read and everywhere proclaimed through the Gospel, as it is declared, in Revelation 5:5, where the Lamb of God alone is able to open the book with the seven seals, which no one else could open, neither in heaven, nor on earth, nor under the earth.

I. CHRIST'S FIRST TITLE OF HONOR AND ATTRIBUTE: HE IS THE WORD

3. That this Gospel may be clearer and more easily understood, we must go back to the passages in the Old Testament upon which it is founded, namely, the beginning of the first chapter of Genesis. There we read, in Genesis 1:1–3, "In the beginning God created the heavens and the earth, and the earth was waste and void; and darkness was upon the face of the deep; and the Spirit of God moved upon the face of the waters. And God said, Let there be light, and there was light," etc. Moses continues how all things were created in like manner as the light, namely, by speaking, or the Word of God. Thus, "And God said, Let there be a firmament." And again, "God said, Let there be sun, moon, stars," etc.

4. From these words of Moses, it is clearly proved that God has a Word, through which or by means of which he spoke, before anything was created; and this Word does not and cannot be anything that was created, since all things were created through this divine utterance, as the text of Moses clearly and forcibly expresses it, when it says, "God said, Let there be light, and there was light." The Word must, therefore, have preceded the light, since light came by the Word; consequently, it was also before all other creatures, which also came by the Word, as Moses writes.

5. But let us go further. If the Word preceded all creatures, and all creatures came by the Word and were created through it, the Word must be a

different being than a creature, and was not made or created like a creature. It must, therefore, be eternal and without beginning. For when all things began, it was already there, and cannot be confined in time nor in creation, but is above time and creation; yea, time and creation are made and have their beginning through it. Thus it follows that whatever is not temporal must be eternal; and that which has no beginning cannot be temporal; and that which is not a creature must be God. For besides God and his creatures, there is nothing. Hence we learn from this text of Moses, that the Word of God, which was in the beginning and through which all things were made and spoken, must be God eternal and not a creature.

6. Again, the Word and he that speaks it, are not one person; for it is not possible that the speaker is himself the Word. What sort of speaker would he be who is himself the Word? He must needs be a mute, or the word must needs sound of itself without the speaker. But Scripture here speaks in strong and lucid words, "God said." And thus God and his Word must be two distinct things.

If Moses had written, "There was an utterance," it would not be so evident that there were two, the Word and the Speaker. But when he says, "God said," and names the speaker and his word, he forcibly states that there are two; that the speaker is not the word, and the word is not the speaker, but that the word comes from the speaker, and has its existence not of itself but from the speaker. But the speaker does not come from the word, nor does he have his existence from it, but from himself. Thus the words of Moses point conclusively to the fact that there are two persons in the Godhead from eternity, before all creatures, that the one has its existence from the other, and the first has its existence from nothing but itself.

7. Again, the Scriptures firmly and everlastingly maintain that there is only one God, as Moses begins, saying, "In the beginning God created the heavens and the earth." And, in Deuteronomy 6:4, "Hear, O Israel; Jehovah our God is one God." Thus the Scriptures proceed in simple, comprehensible words, and teach such exalted things so plainly that everyone may well understand them, and so forcibly that no one can gainsay them. Who is there that cannot here understand from these words of Moses, that there must be two persons in the Godhead, and yet but one God, unless he wishes to deny the plain Scriptures?

8. Again, who is there so subtle as to be able to contradict this doctrine? He must distinguish or keep apart the Word from God, the speaker; and he must confess that it was before all creatures, and that the creatures were made by it. Consequently, he must surely admit it to be God for, besides the creatures, there is nothing but God; he must also admit that there is only one

God. Thus the Scriptures forcibly conclude that these two persons are one perfect God, and that each one is the only true, real, and perfect God, who has created all things; that the Speaker has his being not from the Word, but that the Word has its being from the Speaker, yet he has his being eternally and from eternity, and outside of all creation.

9. The Arian heretics intended to draw a mist over this clear passage and to bore a hole into heaven, since they could not surmount it, and said that this Word of God was indeed God, not by nature, however, but by creation. They said that all things were created by it, but it had also been created previously, and after that all things were created by it. This they said from their own imagination without any authority from the Scriptures, because they left the simple words of the Scriptures and followed their own fancies.

10. Therefore, I have said that he who desires to proceed safely on firm ground, must have no regard for the many subtle and hair-splitting words and fancies, but must cling to the simple, powerful, and explicit words of Scripture, and he will be secure. We shall also see how Saint John anticipated these same heretics and refuted them in their subterfuges and fabrications.

11. Therefore, we have here in the books of Moses the real gold mine, from which everything that is written in the New Testament concerning the divinity of Christ has been taken. Here you may see from what source the Gospel of Saint John is taken, and upon what it is founded; and, therefore, it is easy to understand.

This is the source of the passage, in Psalm 33:6, "By the Word of Jehovah the heavens were made." Solomon in beautiful words describes the wisdom of God, in Proverbs 3:22, saying that this wisdom had been in God before all things; and he takes his thoughts from this chapter of Moses. So almost all the prophets have worked in this mine and have dug their treasures from it.

12. But there are other passages by this same Moses concerning the Holy Ghost as, for example, in Genesis 1:22, "And the Spirit of God moved upon the face of the waters." Thus the Spirit of God must also be something different from him who breathes him into existence, sends him forth, and yet he must be before all creatures.

Again, Moses says in Genesis 1:28–31, "God blessed the creatures, beheld them, and was pleased with them." This benediction and favorable contemplation of the creatures point to the Holy Ghost, since the Scriptures attribute to him life and mercy. But these passages are not so well developed as those which refer to the Son; consequently, they are not so prominent. The ore is still halfway in the mines, so that these passages can easily be believed, if reason is so far in subjection as to believe that there are two persons. If anyone will take the time and trouble to compare the passages of the New Testament referring to the Holy Ghost with this text of Moses, he will find much light, as well as pleasure.

13. Now we must open wide our hearts and understanding, so as to look upon these words not as the insignificant, perishable words of man, but think of them as being as great as he is who speaks them. It is a Word which he speaks of himself, which remains in him, and is never separated from him.

Therefore, according to the thought of the apostle, we must consider how God speaks with himself and to himself, and how the Word proceeds from within himself. However, this Word is not an empty sound, but brings with it the whole essence of the divine nature. Reference has been made in the Epistle to the brightness of his glory and the image of his person, which constitute the divine nature, so that it accompanies the image in its entirety and thus becomes the very image itself. In the same manner, God of himself also utters his Word, so that the whole Godhead accompanies the Word and in its nature remains in, and essentially is, the Word.

14. Behold, here we see whence the apostle has taken his language, when he calls Christ an image of the divine essence, and the brightness of divine glory. He takes it from this text of Moses, when he says that God spoke the Word of himself; this can be nothing else than an image that represents him, since every word is a sign which means something. But here the thing signified is by its very nature in the sign or in the Word, which is not in any other sign. Therefore, he very properly calls it a real image or sign of his nature.

15. The word of man may also in this connection be used in a measure as an illustration; for by it the human heart is known. Thus we commonly say, I understand his heart or intentions, when we have only heard his words; as out of the fullness of the heart the mouth speaks, and from the word the heart is known, as though it were in the word. In consequence of this experience, the heathen had a saying, *Qualis quisque est talia loquitur* (As a man speaks, so is he.). Again, *Oratio est character animi* (Speech is an image of the heart.). When the heart is pure, it utters pure words; when it is impure, it utters impure words. With this also corresponds the Gospel of Matthew 12:34, where Christ says, "Out of the abundance of the heart the mouth speaketh." And again, "How can ye, being evil, speak good things?" Also John the Baptist says, in John 3:31, "He that is of the earth is of the earth, and of the earth he speaketh." The Germans also have a proverb: "Of what the heart is full, overfloweth out of the mouth." The bird is known by its song, for it sings according to its nature. Therefore, all the world knows that nothing represents

the condition of the heart so perfectly and so positively as the words of the mouth, just as though the heart were in the word.

16. Thus it is also with God. His Word is so much like himself, that the Godhead is wholly in it, and he who has the Word has the whole Godhead. But this comparison has its limits. For the human word does not carry with it the essence or the nature of the heart, but simply its meaning, or is a sign of the heart, just as a woodcut or a bronze tablet does not carry with it the human being, but simply represents it. But here in God, the Word does not only carry with it the sign and picture, but the whole being, and is as full of God as he whose word or picture it is. If the human word were pure heart, or the intention of the heart, the comparison would be perfect. But this cannot be; consequently, the Word of God is above every word, and without comparison among all creatures.

17. There have indeed been sharp discussions about the inner word in the heart of man, which remains within, since man has been created in the image of God. But it is all so deep and mysterious, and will ever remain so, that it is not possible to understand it. Therefore, we shall pass on, and we come now to our Gospel, which is in itself clear and manifest.

In the beginning was the Word.

18. What beginning does the evangelist mean except the one of which Moses says, "In the beginning God created the heavens and the earth"? That was the beginning and origin of creation. Other than this, there was no beginning, for God had no beginning, but is eternal. It follows, therefore, that the Word is also eternal, because it did not have its origin in the beginning, but it was already in the beginning, John says. It did not begin, but when other things began it was already in existence; and its existence did not begin when all things began, but it was then already present.

19. How prudently the evangelist speaks, for he does not say, "In the beginning the Word was made," but it was there, and was not made. The origin of its existence is different from the beginning of creation. Furthermore, he says, "In the beginning." Had he been made before the world, as the Arians maintain, he would not have been in the beginning, but he would have himself been the beginning. But John firmly and clearly maintains, "In the beginning was the Word," and he was not the beginning. Whence has Saint John these words? From Moses, in Genesis 1:3, "God said, Let there be light." From this text, evidently, come the words, "In the beginning was the Word." For if God spoke, there had to be a Word. And if he spoke it in the beginning, when the creation began, it was already in the beginning, and did not begin with the creation.

20. But why does he not say, Before the beginning was the Word? This would have made the matter clearer, as it would seem; thus Saint Paul often says, Before the creation of the world, etc. The answer is, because, to be in the beginning, and to be before the beginning, are the same, and one is the consequence of the other. Saint John, as an evangelist, wished to agree with the writings of Moses, wished to open them up, and to disclose the source of his own words, which would not have been the case had he said, "Before" the beginning. Moses says nothing of that which was before the beginning, but describes the Word in the beginning, in order that he can the better describe the creation, which was made by the Word. For the same reason, he also calls him a word, when he might as well have called him a light, life, or something else, as is done later; for Moses speaks of a word. Now, not to begin and to be in the beginning are the same as to be before the beginning.

But if the Word had been in the beginning and not before the beginning, it must have begun to be before the beginning, and so the beginning would have been before the beginning, which would be a contradiction, and would be the same as though the beginning were not the beginning. Therefore, it is put in a masterly way, In the beginning was the Word, so as to show that it has not begun and, consequently, must necessarily have been eternal, before the beginning.

And the Word was with God.

21. Where else should it have been? There never was anything outside of God. Moses says the same thing when he writes, "God said, Let there be light." Whenever God speaks, the Word must be with him. But here he clearly distinguishes the persons, so that the Word is a different person than God with whom it was. This passage of John does not allow the interpretation that God had been alone, because it says that something had been with God, namely, the Word. If he had been alone, why would he need to say, The Word was with God? To have something with him, is not to be alone or by himself.

It should not be forgotten that the evangelist strongly emphasizes the little word "with," for he repeats it, and clearly expresses the difference in persons to gainsay natural reason and future heretics. For while natural reason can understand that there is but one God, and many passages of Scripture substantiate it, and this is also true, yet the Scriptures also strongly oppose the idea that this same God is only one person.

22. Thus arose the heresy of Sabellius, who said, The Father, Son, and Holy Ghost are only one person. And again, Arius, although he admitted that

the Word was with God, would not admit that he was true God. The former confesses and teaches too great a simplicity of God; the latter too great a multiplicity. The former mingles the persons; the latter separates the natures. But the true Christian faith takes the mean, teaches and confesses separate persons and an undivided nature. The Father is a different person from the Son, but he is not another God. Natural reason cannot comprehend this; it must be apprehended by faith alone. Natural reason produces error and heresy; faith teaches and maintains the truth, for it clings to the Scriptures, which do not deceive nor lie.

And God was the Word.

23. Since there is but one God, it must be true that God himself is the Word, which was in the beginning before all creation. Some change the order of the words and read, And the Word was God, in order to explain that this Word not only is with God and is a different person, but that it is also in its essence the one true God with the Father. But we shall leave the words in the order in which they now stand: And God was the Word; and this is also what it means; there is no other God than the one only God, and this same God must also essentially be the Word, of which the evangelist speaks; so there is nothing in the divine nature which is not in the Word. It is clearly stated that this Word is truly God, so that it is not only true that the Word is God, but also that God is the Word.

24. Decidedly, as this passage opposes Arius, who teaches that the Word is not God, so strongly it appears to favor Sabellius, for it speaks as though it mingled the persons, and thereby revokes or explains away the former passage, which separates the persons and says, The Word was with God.

But the evangelist intentionally arranged his words so as to refute all heretics. Here, therefore, he overthrows Arius and attributes to the Word the true essential of the Godhead by saying, And God was the Word; as though he would say, I do not simply say, the Word is God, which might be understood as though the Godhead was only asserted of him, and were not essentially his, as you, Arius, claim; but I say, And God was the Word, which can be understood in no other way than that this same being which everyone calls God and regards as such, is the Word.

Again, that Sabellius and reason may not think that I side with them, and mingle the persons, and revoke what I have said on this point, I repeat it and say again,

The same was in the beginning with God.

25. The Word was with God, with God, and yet God was the Word. Thus the evangelist contends that both assertions are true: God is the Word, and the Word is with God; one nature of divine essence, and yet not one person only. Each person is God complete and entire, in the beginning and eternally. These are the passages upon which our faith is founded and to which we must hold fast. For it is entirely above reason that there should be three persons and each one perfect and true God, and yet not three Gods but one God.

26. The Scholastics have argued much pro and con with their numerous subtleties to make this doctrine comprehensible. But if you do not wish to become entangled in the meshes of the enemy, ignore their cunning, arrogance, and subtleties, and hold to these divine words. Press into them and remain in them, like a hare in a rocky crevice. If you come out and deign to listen to human talk, the enemy will lead you on and overcome you, so that you will at last not know where reason, faith, God, or even yourself are.

27. Believe me, as one who has experienced and tried it, and who does not talk into an empty barrel, the Scriptures are not given us for naught. If reason could have kept on the right road, the Scriptures would not have been given us. Take an example in the case of Arius and Sabellius. Had they clung to the Scriptures and disregarded reason, they would not have originated so much trouble in the church. And our Scholastics might have been Christians, had they ceased fooling with their subtleties and had clung to the Scriptures.

All things were made through him.

28. Has this not been put clearly enough? Who would be surprised, if stubborn men reject every effort to convince them of their error, however plainly and earnestly the truth may be told them, when the Arians could evade this clear and explicit passage and say, All things are made by the Word, but the Word was itself first made, and afterward all things were made by it? And this in opposition to the direct words, "All things were made through him." And there is no doubt that he was not made and cannot be counted among the things that were made. For he who mentions all things excludes nothing, as Saint Paul also explains Psalm 8:6, when he says, in Hebrews 2:8, "Thou didst put all things in subjection under his feet. For in that he subjected all things unto him, he left nothing that is not subjected to him." Again, in 1 Corinthians 15:27, "For he put all things in subjection under his feet. It is evident that he is expected who did subject all things unto him."

So also the words, "All things were made through him," must certainly be understood to except him by whom all things were made, and without whom is nothing that is made. This passage is also based upon the first chapter of

Genesis, where all created things are mentioned which God had made, and in each case it is said, "And God said, and it was so," in order to show that they were all made by the Word. But Saint John continues and explains himself still more fully when he says,

And without him was not anything made that hath been made.

29. If nothing was made without him, much less is he himself made without whom nothing was made; accordingly, the error of Arius should never have attracted any attention, and yet it did. There is no need of comment to explain that the Word is God and the real Creator of all created things, since without him nothing was made that ever was made.

30. Some have been in doubt about the order of the words in this text; the words "that was made" they take with the following words, in this way, "That which was made, was in him life." Of this opinion was Saint Augustine. But the words properly belong to the preceding words as I have given them, thus, "And without him was not anything made that hath been made." He means to say that none of the things that are made, are made without him; so that he may the more clearly express that all things were made through him, and that he himself was not made. In short, the evangelist firmly maintains that the Word is true God, yet not of himself, but of the Father. Therefore, we say, Made through him, and begotten of the Father.

II. CHRIST'S SECOND TITLE OF HONOR AND ATTRIBUTE: IN HIM WAS LIFE

31. On this passage there is generally much speculation, and it is often taken to mean something hard to understand in reference to the twofold existence of creation; in this, the Platonic philosophers are famous. They maintain that all creation has its being first in its own nature and kind, as it was created. Secondly, all creation has its being in divine Providence from eternity, in that he has resolved in himself to create all things. Therefore, as he lives so all things are living in him; and this creative existence in God, they say, is nobler than the existence in its own kind and nature. For in God things do live which in themselves have no life, as stones, earth, water, and the like.

And therefore Saint Augustine says that this Word is an image of all creation, and like a bedchamber is hung with images which are called Ideas (Greek for images), according to which the created things were made, each one according to its own image. Concerning these, John is to have said, "In him was life." Then they connect these words with the preceding ones, thus,

That which was made was life in him, that is, all that was ever created, before it was created, had had its life in him.

32. But this is going too far and is a forced interpretation of this passage. For John speaks very simply and plainly, and does not mean to lead us into such hair-splitting, subtle contemplations. I do not know that the Scriptures anywhere speak of created beings in this way. They do say that all things were known, elected, and even ready and living in the sight of God, as though creation had already taken place, as Christ says of Abraham, Isaac, and Jacob in Luke 20:38, "He (God) is not the God of the dead, but of the living; for all live unto him." But we do not find it written in this sense that all things live in him.

33. This passage also implies something more than the life of the creature, which was in him before the world. It signifies in the simplest manner that he is the fountain and cause of life, that all things which live, live by him and through him and in him, and besides him there is no life, as he himself says, in John 14:6, "I am the way, the truth, and the life." Again, in John 11:25, "I am the resurrection and the life." Consequently, John calls him in 1 John 1:1, "The Word of Life"; and he speaks especially of the life which man receives by him, that is, eternal life; and it was for this very life that John set out to write his Gospel.

34. This is also apparent from the context. For he himself explains the life of which he speaks, when he says, "And the life was the light of men." By these words, he undoubtedly shows that he speaks of the life and the light Christ gives to man through himself. For this reason also, he refers to John the Baptist as a witness of that light. It is, therefore, evident how John the Baptist preached Christ, not in lofty terms of speculation, as some fable; but he taught in a plain, simple way how Christ is the light and the life of all men for their salvation.

35. Therefore, it is well to remember that John wrote his Gospel, as the historians tell us, because Cerinthus, the heretic, arose in his day and taught that Christ did not exist before his mother Mary, thus making a simple human being or creature of him. In opposition to this heretic, he begins his Gospel in an exalted tone and continues thus to the end, so that in almost every letter he preaches the divinity of Christ, which is done by none of the other evangelists. And so he also purposely introduces Christ as acting strangely toward his mother and, "Woman, what have I to do with thee?" he said to her, in John 2:4. Was not this a strange, harsh expression for a son to use in addressing his mother? So also on the cross he said, "Woman, behold thy son," in John 19:26. All this he does in order to set forth Christ as true God over against Cerinthus;

and this he does in language so as not only to meet Cerinthus, but also Arius, Sabellius, and all other heretics.

36. We read also that this same pious John saw Cerinthus in a bathing house and said to his followers, "Let us flee quickly hence that we be not destroyed with this man." And after John had come out, the bathing house is said to have collapsed and destroyed this enemy of the truth. He thus points and directs all his words against the error of Cerinthus, and says, Christ was not only before his mother, nay, he was in the beginning the Word of which Moses writes in the very beginning, and all things were made by him, and he was with God and the Word was God, and was in the beginning with God; and thus he strikes Cerinthus as with thunderbolts.

37. Thus we take the meaning of the evangelist in this passage to be simply and plainly this: He who does not recognize and believe Christ to be true God, as I have so far described him, that he was the Word in the beginning with God, and that all things were made by him, but wishes to make him only a creature of time, coming after his mother, as Cerinthus teaches, is eternally lost, and cannot attain to eternal life; for there is no life without this Word and Son of God; in him alone is life. The man Christ, separate from, and without, God, would be useless, as he says himself in John 6:55, 63, "The flesh profiteth nothing. My flesh is meat indeed, and my blood is drink indeed."

Why does the flesh profit nothing, and yet my flesh is the only true meat? The plain reason is, because I am not mere flesh and simply man, but I am God's son. My flesh is meat not because it is flesh, but because it is my flesh. This is as much as to say, He who believes that I, who am man, and have flesh and blood like other men, am the Son of God, and God, finds in me true nourishment, and will live. But he who believes me to be only man, is not profited by the flesh, for to him it is not my flesh or God's flesh.

He also says, "Ye shall die in your sins, except ye believe that I am he," in John 8:24. Again, "If the son shall therefore make you free, ye shall be free indeed." This is also the meaning of the following passage, "In him was life." The Word of God in the beginning, who is himself God, must be our life, meat, light, and salvation. Therefore, we cannot attribute to Christ's human nature the power of making us alive, but the life is in the Word, which dwells in the flesh and makes us alive by the flesh.

38. This interpretation is simple and helpful. Thus Saint Paul is wont to call the doctrine of the Gospel "*doctrina pietatis,*" a doctrine of piety—a doctrine that makes men rich in grace. However, the other interpretation which the heathen also have, namely, that all creatures live in God, does indeed make subtle disputants and is obscure and difficult; but it teaches nothing

about grace, nor does it make men rich in grace. Wherefore, the Scriptures speak of it as "idle."

Just as we interpret the words of Christ, when he says, "I am the life," so also should we interpret these words, and say nothing philosophically of the life of the creatures in God; but on the contrary, we should consider how God lives in us, and makes us partakers of his life, so that we live through him, of him, and in him. For it cannot be denied that through him natural life also exists, which even unbelievers have from him, as Saint Paul says, "In him we live, and move, and have our being; for we are also his offspring," in Acts 17:28.

39. Yes, natural life is a part of eternal life, its beginning, but on account of death it has an end, because it does not acknowledge and honor him from whom it comes; sin cuts it off so that it must die forever. On the other hand, those who believe in him, and acknowledge him from whom they have their being, shall never die; but this natural life of theirs will be extended into eternal life, so that they will never taste death, as John says, in John 8:51, "Verily, verily, I say unto you, if a man keep my word, he shall never see death." And again, in John 11:25, "He that believeth on me, though he die, yet shall he live." These and similar passages are well understood when we rightly learn to know Christ, how he has slain death and has brought us life.

40. But when the evangelist says, "In him was life," and not, "In him is life," as though he spoke of things past, the words must not be taken to mean the time before creation, or the time of the beginning; for he does not say, "In the beginning life was in him," as he has just before said of the Word, which was in the beginning with God; but these words must be referred to the time of Christ's life or sojourn upon earth, when the Word of God appeared to men and among men; for the evangelist proposes to write about Christ and that life in which he accomplished all things necessary for our life. Just as he says of John the Baptist, "There came a man, sent from God"; and again, "He was not the Light, etc."; even so, he afterward speaks of the Word, "And the Word became flesh, and dwelt among us"; "He was in the world"; "He came unto his own, and they that were his own received him not"; etc. In the same manner does Christ also speak of John the Baptist, "He was the lamp that burneth and shineth," in John 5:35.

41. So he says also here, "In him was life"; and Christ says of himself, "When I am in the world, I am the light of the world," in John 9:5. The words of the evangelist, therefore, simply refer to the sojourn of Christ on earth. For as I said at first, this Gospel is not as difficult as some think; it has been made difficult by their looking for great, mysterious, and mighty things in it. The evangelist has written it for ordinary Christians, and has made his

words perfectly intelligible. For whoever will disregard the life and sojourn of Christ upon earth, and will wish to find him in some other way, as he now sits in heaven, will always fail. He must look for him as he was and as he sojourned while upon earth, and he will then find life. Here Christ was made our life, light, and salvation; here all things occurred that we are to believe concerning him. It has really been said in a most befitting manner, "In him was life," not, that he is not our life now, but that he does not now do that which he then did.

42. That this is the meaning can be seen from the words of the text when it says, "John the Baptist came for witness, that he might bear witness of the light, that all might believe through him." It is sufficiently clear that John came solely to bear witness of Christ, and yet he has said nothing at all of the life of the creatures in God supporting the above philosophical interpretation; but all his teaching and preaching were concerning the life of Christ upon earth, whereby he became the Life and Light of men. Now follows:

III. CHRIST'S THIRD TITLE OF HONOR AND ATTRIBUTE: HE WAS THE LIGHT

A. Christ Was the Light of Men

And the Life was the Light of men.

43. Just as the word "life" was interpreted differently from the meaning intended by the evangelist, so was also the word "light." There has been much foolish speculation as to how the Word of God in its divinity could be a light, which naturally shines and has always given light to the minds of men even among the heathen. Therefore, the light of reason has been emphasized and based upon this passage of Scripture.

44. These are all human, Platonic, and philosophical thoughts, which lead us away from Christ into ourselves; but the evangelist wishes to lead us away from ourselves into Christ. For he would not deal with the divine, almighty, and eternal Word of God, nor speak of it, otherwise than as flesh and blood, that sojourned upon earth. He would not have us diffuse our thoughts among the creatures which he has created, so as to pursue him, search for him, and speculate about him as the Platonic philosophers do; but he wishes to lead us away from those vague and high-flown thoughts and bring us together in Christ.

The evangelist means to say, Why do you make such extensive excursions and search for him so far away? Behold, in the man Christ are all things. He has made all things; in him is life, and he is the Word by whom all things were made. Remain in him and you will find all; he is the life and the light of all men. Whoever directs you elsewhere, deceives you. For he has offered himself in this flesh and blood, and he must be sought and will be found there. Follow the testimony of John the Baptist; he will show you no other life or light than this man, who is God himself. Therefore, this light must mean the true light of grace in Christ, and not the natural light, which also sinners, Jews, heathen, and devils have, who are the greatest enemies of the light.

45. But let no one accuse me of teaching differently from Saint Augustine, who interpreted this text to mean the natural light. I do not reject that interpretation, and am well aware that all the light of reason is ignited by the divine light; and as I have said of the natural life, that it has its origin in, and is a part of, the true life, when it has come to the right knowledge, so also the light of reason has its origin in, and is part of, the true light, when it recognizes and honors him by whom it has been ignited.

It, however, does not do this of itself, but remains separate and by itself, becomes perverted, and likewise perverts all things; therefore, it must become extinguished and die out. But the light of grace does not destroy the natural light. To the light of nature, it is quite clear that two and three make five. That the good is to be encouraged and the evil avoided is also clear to it; and thus the light of grace does not extinguish the light of nature, but the latter never gets so far as to be able to distinguish the good from the evil. It is with him as one who wishes to go to Rome with Rome behind his back; for he himself well knew that whoever would go to Rome must travel the right way, but he knew not which was the right road. So it is also with the natural light; it does not take the right road to God, nor does it know or recognize the right way, although it knows well that one must get on the right road. Thus reason always prefers the evil to the good; it would never do this if it fully realized with a clear vision that the good only should be chosen.

46. But this interpretation is out of place in this connection, because only the light of grace is preached here. Saint Augustine was only a man, and we are not compelled to follow his interpretation, since the text here clearly indicates that the evangelist speaks of the light of which John the Baptist bore witness, which is ever the light of grace, even Christ himself.

47. And since this is an opportunity, we shall further describe this deceptive natural light, which causes so much trouble and misfortune. This natural light is like all the other members and powers of man. Who doubts that man with all his powers has been created by the eternal Word of God like all other things, and is a creature of God? But yet there is no good in him, as Moses

says, in Genesis 6:5, "Every imagination of the thoughts of man's heart was only evil continually."

48. Although the flesh was created by God, yet it is not inclined to chastity, but to unchastity. Although the heart was created by God, it is not inclined to humility, nor to the love of one's neighbor, but to pride and selfishness, and it acts according to this inclination, where it is not forcibly restrained. So it is with the natural light; although it is naturally so bright as to know that only good is to be done, it is so perverted that it is never sure as to what is good; it calls good whatever is pleasing to itself, is taken up with it, and only concludes to do what it has selected as good. Thus it continues to pursue the evil instead of the good.

49. We shall prove this by examples. Reason knows very well that we ought to be pious and serve God; of this it knows how to talk, and thinks it can easily beat all the world. Very well, this is true and well said; but when it is to be done, and reason is to show how and in what way we are to be pious and serve God, it knows nothing, is purblind, and says one must fast, pray, sing, and do the works of the law; it continues to act the fool with works, until it has gone so far astray as to imagine that people are serving God in building churches, ringing bells, burning frankincense, whining, singing, wearing hoods, shaving their heads, burning candles, and other innumerable tomfoolery, of which all the world is now full and more than full. In this monstrously blind error, reason continues, even while the bright light shines on, that enjoins piety and service to God.

50. When now Christ, the light of grace, comes and also teaches that we are to be pious and serve God, he does not extinguish this natural light, but opposes the way and manner of becoming pious and serving God as taught by reason. He says, To become pious is not to do works; no works are good without faith.

51. Then begins the fight. Reason rises up against grace, and cries out against its light, accuses it of forbidding good works, protests against not having its own way and standard of becoming pious, being thus set aside; but continually rages about being pious and serving God, and so makes the light of grace foolishness, nay, error and heresy, and persists in persecuting and banishing it. See, this is the virtue of the light of nature, that it raves against the true light, is constantly boasting of piety, piety, and is always crying, "Good works!" "Good works!" but it cannot and will not stand to be taught what piety is and what good works are; it insists that which it thinks and proposes must be right and good.

52. Behold, here then you have the cause and origin of all idolatry, of all heresy, of all hypocrisy, of all error, of which all the prophets have spoken, on account of which they were killed, and against which all the Scriptures protest.

All this comes from the stubborn, self-willed arrogance and delusion of natural reason, which is self-confident and puffed up because it knows that we ought to be pious, and serve God; it will neither listen to, nor suffer, a teacher to teach them, thinks it knows enough, and would find out for itself what it is to be pious and serve God, and how it may do so. Therefore, divine truth cannot and must not submit to reason; for this would be the greatest mistake and be contrary to God's honor and glory. In this way, contentions and tribulations arise.

53. Therefore, it is clear, I think, that John does not speak here of the false light, nor of that bright natural light, which rightly claims that we must be pious, for it is already here, and Christ did not come to bring it, but to dim and blind this false, self-willed arrogance, and to set in its place the light of grace, to wit, faith. And this also the words themselves indicate, when they say, "The life was the light of men." If it is the light of men, it must be a different light from the one that is in men, since man already has the light of nature in him, and whatever enlightens man, enlightens the light of nature in man, and brings another light, which surpasses the light that is in man.

He does not say that it is the light of irrational animals, but of man, who is a rational being. For there is not a man found in whom there is not the natural light of reason, from which cause alone he is called man and is worthy to be a man. If the evangelist would have us understand by this light the natural light of reason, he would have said, The life was a light of darkness; as Moses writes in Genesis 1:2, "And darkness was upon the face of the deep." Therefore, this light must be that which was revealed in Christ on earth.

54. Notice also the order of the words. John puts the Life before the Light. He does not say, "The light was the life of men" but, on the contrary, "The life was the light of men," for the reason that in Christ there is reality and truth, and not simply appearance as in men. Saint Luke speaks of Christ's external life thus, in Luke 24:19, "He was a prophet mighty in deed and word" and in Acts 1:1, "Jesus began both to do and teach," where "doing" precedes the "teaching"; for where there is only teaching without doing, there is hypocrisy. Thus John says of John the Baptist, "He was the lamp that burneth and shineth," in John 5:35; for to be simply shining and not burning is deceptive. In order, therefore, that Christ may here also be recognized as the true, unerring

light, John says that all things were life in him, and this same life afterward
was the light of men.

55. It follows then that man has no other light than Christ, God's son in
the flesh. And whosoever believes that Christ is true God, and that in him is
life, will be illumined and quickened by this life. The light supports him, so
that he may remain where Christ is. As the Godhead is an eternal life, this
same light is an eternal light; and as this same life can never die, so also this
light can never be extinguished; and faith in it cannot perish.

56. We may also especially notice that the evangelist assigns life to Christ,
as the eternal Word, and not to Christ the man; for he says, "In him," emi-
nently in the Word, "was the life." Although Christ died as man, yet he ever
remained alive; for life could not and cannot die; and consequently, death was
overcome and was swallowed up in life, so much so that his humanity soon
again became alive.

This same Life is the light of men; for he who recognizes and believes in
such a life in Christ, indeed passes through death, yet never dies, as has been
stated above. For this Light of life protects him, so that death cannot harm
him. Although the body must die and decay, the soul will not feel this death,
because it is in that light, and through that light, that it is entirely compre-
hended in the life of Christ. But he who does not believe this, remains in
darkness and death; and although his body is united to him, even as it will be
forever at the day of judgment, yet the soul will nevertheless taste and feel
death, and will die eternally.

57. From this, we may realize how great was the harm which Cerinthus
threatened, and which all do who believe and teach that Christ is only man
and not true God. For his humanity would profit us nothing if the divinity
were not in it. Yet, on the other hand, God will not and cannot be found, save
through and in his humanity, which he has set up as an ensign for the nations,
gathering together the dispersed of Judah from the four corners of the earth,
in Isaiah 11:12.

58. See now, if you will believe that in Christ there is such life that remains
even in death, and has overcome death, this light will lighten you aright, and
will remain a light and life within you even at the time of your death. It follows
then that such Life and Light cannot be mere creatures, for no creature can
overcome death, either in itself or in another. Behold, how easy and becoming this interpretation of the light is, and how much better it is for our salvation; but how very far they are from it who wish to make of this light only
the natural light of reason. For this latter light does not improve anyone, nay,
it leads only farther away from Christ into creation and to false reason. We

must enter into Christ, and not look at the lights which come from him, but gaze at his light, which is the origin of all lights. We must follow the streams which lead to the source and not away from it.

B. Christ Was the Light That Shineth in the Darkness

And the light shineth in the darkness
and the darkness apprehended it not.

59. This passage has also been interpreted with such lofty ideas, and made to mean that reason has a natural light, as I have just mentioned, and that the same is kindled by God; and yet reason does not recognize, understand, nor feel him, the real Light, by whom it is kindled; therefore, it is in darkness, and does not behold the Light from which nevertheless it receives all its vision.

60. Oh, that this interpretation, that reason has a natural light, were rooted out of my heart! How deeply it is seated there. Not that it is false or wrong in itself, but because it is out of place and untimely in this Gospel connection, and it will not allow these blessed and comforting words of the Gospel to remain simple and pure in their true meaning. Why do they not thus speak also of the natural life? For even the natural life is surely quickened by the divine life, just as much as the light of reason is kindled by the divine light.

They might just as well say that life quickens the dead and the dead apprehend it not, as to say that the light illumines dark reason and reason apprehends it not. I might also say that the eternal will makes the unwilling willing, and the unwilling do not apprehend it; and in like manner we might speak of all our other natural gifts and powers. But how does reason and its light fall on such speculations? The Platonic philosophers with their useless and senseless prating first led Augustine to his interpretation. The glitter was so fascinating that they were even called the divine philosophers. Augustine then carried us all with him.

61. What more can their talk teach than this, that reason is illumined by God, who is inconceivable and incomprehensible light? Just so, life is given by God, who is inconceivable life, and all our powers are made powerful by God, who is inconceivable power. And as he is near to the light of reason with his inconceivable life, and to the powers with his inconceivable power, as Saint Paul says, "In him we live, and move, and have our being," in Acts 17:28. Again, "Am I a God at hand, saith Jehovah, and not a God afar off? Do not I fill heaven and earth?" in Jeremiah 23:23, 24.

Thus we have just heard in the Epistle that "He upholds all things by the word of his power," in Hebrews 1:3. Therefore, he is not only near to the light of reason and illumines it, but he is near also to all creatures, and flows and pours into them, shines and works in them, and fills all things. Accordingly, we are not to think that Saint John speaks here of the light of reason; he simply sets mankind before him, and tells what kind of light they have in Christ, aside from and above the light of nature.

62. It is also a blind and awkward expression to say of the natural light that the darkness apprehended it not. What else would this be than to say that reason is illumined and kindled by the divine light, and yet, remains in darkness and receives no light? Whence comes this natural light? There can never be darkness where a light is kindled; although there is darkness from the want of the light of grace. But here they are not speaking of the light of grace, and so they cannot refer to like or spiritual darkness. Therefore, it is a contradiction of terms to say that the light illumined the darkness, and the darkness apprehended it not, or the darkness remained. One might as well say that life is given to a dead person, and the dead person does not apprehend it nor receive it, but remains dead.

63. But if someone should say that we are not able to apprehend him who gives light and life, then I really hear, what angel does apprehend him? What saint apprehends the one who offers him grace? Verily he remains concealed and unapprehended: but this does not mean, as the evangelist here says, that the Light is not apprehended in darkness; but as the words read, it means, the Light shines into the darkness, but the darkness remains darkness and is not illuminated; the Light shines upon the darkness, and yet the darkness remains; just as the sun shines upon the blind, and yet they do not perceive it. Behold how many words I must waste in order to remove this foreign and false interpretation of our text!

64. Therefore, let us cling to the simple meaning the words convey when we do no violence to them. All who are illumined by natural reason apprehend the light, each one being illumined according to his talent and capacity. But this Light of grace, which is given to men aside from and above the natural light, shines in darkness, that is, among men of the world, who are blind and without grace; but they do not accept it, yea, they even persecute it. This is what Christ means when he says, in John 3:19, "And as this is the judgment, that the light is come into the world, and men loved the darkness rather than the light." Behold, Christ was upon earth and among men before he was publicly preached by John the Baptist; but no one took notice of him. He was the Life and Light of men. He lived and did shine; yet there was nothing but darkness, and the darkness did not perceive him. Everybody was worldly blind and benighted. Had they apprehended who he was, they would have given him due

honor, as Saint Paul says, "Had the rulers of this world known the wisdom of God, they would not have crucified the Lord of glory," in 1 Corinthians 2:8.

65. Thus Christ has always been the Life and Light, even before his birth, from the beginning, and will ever remain so to the end. He shines at all times in all creatures, in the holy Scriptures, through his saints, prophets, and ministers, in his word and works; and he has never ceased to shine. But in whatever place he has shone, there was great darkness, and the darkness apprehended him not.

66. Saint John may have indeed directed these words thus against the followers of Cerinthus, so that they saw the plain Scriptures and the truth that enlightened them, yet they did not apprehend their darkness. So it is at all times, and even now. Although the Scriptures are explained to blind teachers so that they may apprehend the truth, yet they do not apprehend it, and the fact remains that the light shines in the darkness and the darkness apprehends it not.

67. It is especially to be observed that the evangelist here says the light shines, *phaenei*, that is, it is manifest and present to the eyes in the darkness. But he who receives nothing more from it remains in darkness; just as the sun shines for the blind man, but he does not on that account see any better. So it is the nature of this light that it shines in darkness, but the darkness does not on that account become brighter. In believers, however, it not only shines, but it makes them transparent and seeing, it lives in them, so that it can properly be said that "The life is the light of men." On the other hand, light without life is a shining of darkness; therefore, no light is of any use to unbelievers, for however clear the truth is presented and shown to them, they still remain in darkness.

68. Let us, then, understand all these sayings of the evangelist as common attributes and titles of Christ, which he wishes to have preached in the church as a preface and introduction of that which he proposes to write of Christ in his whole Gospel, namely, that he is true God and true man, who has created all things, and has been given to man as Life and Light, although but a few of all those to whom he is revealed receive him.

This is what our Gospel lesson contains and nothing more. In the same manner, Saint Paul also composes a preface and introduction to his Epistle to the Romans, in Romans 1:1. Now follows the actual beginning of this Gospel:

C. Christ Was the Light of Which John Bore Witness

There came a man, sent from God, whose name was John.

69. Saint Mark and Saint Luke begin their Gospels with John the Baptist, and they should begin with him; as Christ himself says, "From the days of

John the Baptist until now the kingdom of heaven suffereth violence," in Matthew 11:12. And Saint Peter says that Jesus began from the baptism of John, by whom he was also called and ordained to be a minister, in Acts 1:22. And Saint John the Baptist himself testifies, "I have beheld the Spirit descending as a dove out of heaven," in John 1:32, and he heard the Father's voice saying, "This is my beloved Son, in whom I am well pleased," in Matthew 3:17. Then Christ was made a teacher, and his public ministry began; then only began the Gospel of Christ. For no one except Christ himself was allowed to begin the exalted, blessed, comforting mission of the Word. And for his sake, John must first come and prepare the people for his preaching, that they might receive the Life and the Light.

70. For, as we have heard, Christ is everywhere the Light which shines in the darkness and is not apprehended; so he was especially and bodily in his humanity present among the Jews, appeared to them; but he was not recognized by them. Therefore, his forerunner, John, came for the sole purpose of preaching him, in order that he might be recognized and received. This passage, therefore, fittingly follows the former one. Since Christ, the shining Light, was not recognized, John came to open the eyes of men and to bear witness of the ever-present, shining light, which afterward was to be received, heard, and recognized itself without the witness of John.

71. It is my opinion that we have now passed through the most difficult and most glorious part of this Gospel; for what is said henceforth is easy, and is the same as that which the other evangelists write of John and of Christ. Although, as I have said, this part is in itself not difficult, yet it has been purposely made so by natural and human interpretations. A passage naturally becomes difficult when a word is taken from its ordinary meaning and given a strange one. Who would not wish to know what a man is, and would not imagine all manner of wonderful things, if he were told that a man is something different from what all the world thinks? This is what happened here to the clear, simple words of the evangelist.

72. Still, John uses a peculiar style, since he always, because of Cerinthus, directs the testimony of John the Baptist to the divinity of Christ, which is not done by the other evangelists, who only refer to Christ, without especially emphasizing his divinity. But here he says, John came to bear witness of the Light, and to preach Christ as the Life, the Light, and as God, as we shall hear.

73. What, therefore, was said about John the Baptist in Advent, is also to be understood here, namely, that, like as he came before Christ and directed the people to him, so the spoken word of the Gospel is simply to preach and point out Christ. It was ordained by God for this purpose alone, just as John

was sent by God. We have also heard that John was a voice in the wilderness, signifying by his office the oral preaching of the Gospel. Since the darkness was of itself unable to apprehend this Light, although it was present, John must needs reveal it and bear witness of it. And even now the natural reason is not able of itself to apprehend it, although it is present in all the world: the oral word of the Gospel must reveal it and proclaim it.

74. We see now that through the Gospel this light is brought to us, not from a distance, nor do we need to go far to obtain it; it is very near us and shines in our hearts; nothing more is needed than that it be pointed out and preached. And he who now hears it preached, and believes, finds it in his heart; for as faith is only in the heart, so also this light is alone in faith. Therefore, I say it is near at hand and within us, but of ourselves we cannot apprehend it; it must be preached and believed. This is also what Saint Paul means when he says, referring to Deuteronomy 30:11–14, "Say not in thine heart, Who shall ascend into heaven? (that is, to bring Christ down), or, Who shall descend into the deep? (that is, to bring Christ up from the dead). But what saith it? The word is nigh thee, in thy mouth, and in thy heart; that is, the word of faith, which we preach," in Romans 10:6–8. Behold this is the light which shines in darkness and is not recognized until John and the Gospel come and reveal it. Then man is enlightened by it, and apprehends it; and yet it changes neither time, nor place, nor person, nor age, but only the heart.

75. Again, as John did not come of himself, but was sent by God, so neither the Gospel nor any sermon on this Light can come of itself or from human reason; but they must be sent by God. Therefore, the evangelist here sets aside all the doctrines of men; for what men teach will never show Christ, the Light, but will only obstruct it. But whatsoever points out Christ is surely sent by God, and has not been invented by man. For this reason, the evangelist mentions the name and says, His name was John. In Hebrew, John means grace or favor, to signify that this preaching and message was not sent on account of any merit of ours; but was sent purely out of God's grace and mercy, and brings to us also God's grace and mercy. Thus Saint Paul says, "How shall they preach, except they be sent?" in Romans 10:15.

76. From all this, we learn that the evangelist speaks of Christ in a manner that he may be recognized as God. For if he is the light which is everywhere present and shines in darkness, and it needs nothing more than that it be revealed through the Word, and recognized in the heart through faith, it must surely be God. No creature can to such a degree be so near in all places, and shine in all hearts. And yet the Light is God in a way as to be still man, and be preached in and by man. The words follow:

The same came for witness, that he might bear witness of the Light,
that all might believe through him.

77. From what has now been said, it is clear that the Gospel proclaims only this Light, the man Christ, and causes the darkness to apprehend it, yet not by reason or feeling, but by faith. For he says, "That all might believe through him." Again, "He came for a witness, that he might bear witness." The nature of bearing witness is that it speaks of that which others do not see, know, or feel; but they must believe him that bears testimony. So also the Gospel does not demand a decision and assent according to reason, but a faith which is above reason, for in no other way can this light be recognized.

78. It was said plainly enough above, in what way the light of reason is in conflict with and rages against this Light, to say nothing of its being adhered to or apprehended by it. For it is positively written, "The darkness apprehendeth the light not"; therefore, reason with its light must be taken captive and blinded; as is said in Isaiah 60:19, "The sun," that is, thy reason, "shall be no more thy light by day; neither for brightness shall the moon give light unto thee; but Jehovah will be unto thee an everlasting light and thy God thy glory," that is, through the Gospel or Word of God, or through the witness of John, which demands faith, and makes a fool of reason. Consequently, witness is borne of this Light through the Word, that reason may keep silent and follow this testimony; then it will apprehend the Light in faith, and its darkness will be illumined. For if reason were able to apprehend this Light of itself, or adhere to it, there would be no need of John or his testimony.

79. Therefore, the aim of the Gospel is to be a witness for reason's sake, which is self-willed, blind, and stubborn. The Gospel resists reason and leads it away from its own light and fancy to faith, through which it can apprehend this living and eternal Light.

He was not the Light, but came that he might bear witness of the Light.

80. Dearly beloved, why does he say this, and repeat the words that John was only a witness of the Light? Oh, what necessary repetition! First of all to show that this Light is not simply a man, but God himself; for, as I have said, the evangelist greatly desires to preach the divinity of Christ in all his words. If John, the great saint, be not that Light, but only a witness of it, then this Light must be something far different from everything that is holy, whether it be man or angel. For if holiness could make such a light, it would have made one of John. But it is above holiness, and must, therefore, be above the angels, who are not more than holy.

81. In the second place, to resist wicked preachers of man, who do not bear witness of Christ, the Light, but of themselves. For it is true indeed, that all who preach the doctrines of men make man the light, lead men away from God to themselves, and set themselves up in the place of the true Light, as the pope and his followers have done. Therefore, he is the Antichrist, that is, he is against Christ, the true Light.

82. This Gospel text allows of no other doctrine beside it; it desires only to testify of Christ and lead men to him, who is the Light. Therefore, O Lord God, these words, "He was not the Light," are truly worthy to be capitalized and to be well remembered against the men who set themselves up as the light and give to men doctrines and laws of their own fabrication. They pretend to enlighten men, but lead them with themselves into the depths of hell; for they do not teach faith, and are not willing to teach it; and no one teaches it except John, who is sent of God, and the holy Gospel. Truly much could be said on this point.

83. In short, he who does not preach the Gospel to you, reject and refuse to hear him. He, however, preaches the Gospel who teaches you to believe and trust in Christ, the eternal Light, and not to build on any of your own works. Therefore, beware of everything told you that does not agree with the Gospel; do not put your trust in it, nor accept it as something external, as you regard eating and drinking, which are necessary for your body, and which you may use at your pleasure or at the pleasure of another; but by no means as something necessary to your salvation. For this purpose nothing is necessary or of use to you except this Light.

84. Oh, these abominable doctrines of men, which are now so prevalent and which have almost banished this Light! They all wish to be this light themselves, but not to be witnesses of it. They advocate themselves and teach their own fancies, but are silent about this Light, or teach it in a way as to preach themselves along with it. This is worse than to be entirely silent; for by such teaching they make Samaritans who partly worship God and partly worship idols, in 2 Kings 17:33.

D. He Was the Light That Lighteth Everyone

There was the true Light, which lighteth every man,
coming into the world.

85. Neither John nor any saint is the Light; but John and all evangelical preachers testify of the true Light. For the present, enough has been said of this Light—what it is, how it is recognized by faith, and how it supports us

eternally in life and death, so that no darkness can ever harm us. But what is remarkable is, that he says, "It lighteth every man, coming into the world." If this be affirmed of the natural light, it would be contradicted when he says that it is "the true Light." He had said before, "The darkness apprehends it not"; and all his words are directed toward the Light of grace. Then follow the words, "He was in the world, and the world knew him not," and "His own received him not." But he whom the true Light lights, is illumined by grace, and recognizes the Light.

86. Again, that he does not speak of the light of grace is evident when he says, "It lighteth every man, coming into the world." This manifestly includes all men who are born into the world. Saint Augustine says it means that no man is illumined except by this Light; it is the same as though we were to say of a teacher in a place where there is no other teacher, This teacher instructs all the city, that is, there is no other teacher in that city; he instructs all the pupils. By it is not said that he teaches all the people in the city, but simply that he is the only teacher in the city, and none are taught but by him.

So here the evangelist would have us know that John is not the Light, nor any man, nor any creature; but that there is only one Light that lights all men, and that no man comes into the world who can possibly be illumined by any other light.

87. And I cannot reject this interpretation; for Saint Paul also speaks in like manner in Romans 5:18, "As through one trespass the judgment came unto all men to condemnation; even so through one act of righteousness the free gift came unto all men unto justification of life." Although all men are not justified through Christ, he is, nevertheless, the only man through whom justification comes.

So it is also here. Although all men are not illumined, nevertheless this is the only light through which all illumination comes. The evangelist has used this manner of speech freely, and had no fear that some might take offense because he says "all men." He thought he would anticipate all such offense, and explains himself before and afterward, and says, "The darkness apprehended him not, and his own received him not." These words are sufficient proof to prevent anyone from saying that the evangelist meant to say that all men are illumined; but he did wish to say that Christ is the only Light that lights all men, and without him no man is lighted.

88. If this were said of the natural light of reason, it would have little significance, since it not only enlightens all men who come into the world, but also those who go out of the world, and even devils. For this light of reason remains in the dead, in devils, and in the condemned, yea, it becomes brighter,

that they may be all the more tormented by it. But since only human beings who come into this world are mentioned, the evangelist indicates that he is speaking of the Light of faith, which lightens and helps only in this life; for after death, no one will be illumined by it. The illuminating must take place in this life through faith in the man Christ, yet by his divinity. After this life, we shall clearly see his divinity without the humanity and without faith.

89. Therefore, the evangelist is careful to form his words so as not by any means to reject the man Christ, and yet so as to declare his divinity. For this reason, it was necessary for him to say "all men," so as to preach only one light for all, and to warn us not to accept in this life the lights of men or any other lights.

One man is not to lighten another, but this light alone is to lighten all men; and ministers are to be only forerunners and witnesses of this Light to men, that all may believe in this Light.

Therefore, when he had said, "Which lighteth every man," he realized that he had said too much, and so he added, "coming into the world," so that he might make Christ the Light of this world. For in the world to come this light will cease and will be changed into eternal glory, as Saint Paul says, "When he shall deliver up the kingdom to God," in 1 Corinthians 15:24; but now he rules through his humanity. When he delivers up the kingdom, he will also deliver up the Light; not as though there were two kinds of light, or as though we were to see something different from what we now see; but we shall see the same Light and the same God we now see in faith, but in a different manner. Now we see him in faith darkly, then we shall see him face to face. Just as though I beheld a gilded picture through a colored glass or veil, and afterward looked at it without these. So also Saint Paul says, "Now we see in a mirror, darkly; but then face to face," in 1 Corinthians 13:12.

90. Behold, you now know of what the evangelist speaks, when he says that Christ is the Light of men through his humanity, that is, in faith, by means of which his divinity is reflected as by a mirror, or is seen as in a glass or as the sun shines through bright clouds. But let us remember that the Light is attributed to his divinity, not to his humanity; and yet his humanity, which is the cloud or curtain before the Light, must not be thought lightly of.

91. This language is sufficiently plain and he who has faith understands very well what is the nature and character of this Light. It matters not if he who does not believe does not understand it. He is not to understand it, for it is better that he knew nothing of the Bible and did not study it, than that he deceive himself and others with his erroneous light; for he imagines it to be the light of Scripture, which, however, cannot be apprehended without true faith. For this Light shines in the darkness, but is not apprehended by it.

92. This passage may also mean that the evangelist has in mind the preaching of the Gospel and of faith in all the world, and so that this Light shines upon all men throughout the world, just as the sun shines upon all men. Saint Paul says, "Be not moved away from the hope of the Gospel which ye heard, which was preached in all creation under heaven," in 1 Colossians 1:23. Christ himself says, "Go ye into all the world, and preach the Gospel to the whole creation," in Mark 16:15. The psalmist also says, "His going forth is from the end of the heavens, and his circuit unto the ends of it; and there is nothing hid from the heat thereof," in Psalm 19:6. How this is to be understood has been explained in the sermon on the Epistle for Christmas, in Isaiah 9:2.

93. By this easy and simple interpretation, we can readily understand how this Light lights every man, coming into the world, so that neither Jews nor anyone else should dare to set up their own light anywhere. And this interpretation is well suited to the preceding passages. For even before John or the Gospel bore witness of the Light, it had shone in darkness and the darkness apprehended it not; but after it has been proclaimed and publicly witnessed to, it shines as far as the world extends, unto all men, although all men will not receive it, as follows:

II. THE COMING OF CHRIST

He was in the world, and the world was made through him,
and the world knew him not.

94. All this is said of Christ as man and refers especially to the time after his baptism, when he began to give light according to John's testimony. He was ever in the world. But what place of the world knew it? Who received him? He was not even received by those with whom he was personally associated, as the following shows:

He came unto his own, and they that were his own received him not.

95. This also is said of his coming as a preacher, and not of his being born into the world. For his coming is his preaching and illumining. The Baptist says, "He it is who coming after me is preferred before me, the latchet of whose shoe I am not worthy to unloose," in Matthew 3:11, Luke 3:16, Mark 1:7, John 1:27. On account of this coming, John is also called his forerunner, as Gabriel said to his father, Zacharias, "He shall go before his face in the spirit and power of Elijah; to make ready for the Lord a people prepared for him," in Luke 1:17. For, as has been said, the Gospels begin with the baptism of Christ. Then he began to be the Light and to do that for which he came. Therefore,

it is said that he came into the world to his own people and his own received him not. If this were not said of his coming to give light by preaching, the evangelist would not thus reprove them for not having received him.

96. Who could know that it was he, if he had not been revealed? Therefore, it is their fault that they did not receive him; for he came and was revealed by John and by himself. Therefore, John says, "That he should be made manifest to Israel, for this cause came I baptizing with water," in John 1:31. And he says himself, "I am come in my Father's name, and ye receive me not; if another shall come in his own name, him ye will receive," in John 5:43. This is also evidently said of the coming of his preaching and of his revelation.

97. He calls the Jews his own people because they were chosen out of all the world to be his people, and he had been promised to them through Abraham, Isaac, Jacob, and David. For to us heathens or gentiles there was no promise of Christ. Therefore, we are strangers and are not called "his own"; but through pure grace we have been adopted, and have thus become his people; though, alas, we also allow him to come daily through the Gospel and do not esteem him. Therefore, we must also suffer that another, the pope, comes in his place and is received by us. We must serve the bitter foe because we will not serve our God.

98. But we must not forget in this connection that the evangelist refers twice to the divinity of Christ. First, when he says, "The world was made through him." Secondly, when he says, "He came unto his own." For it is the nature only of the true God to have his own people. The Jews were always God's own people, as the Scriptures frequently declare. If, then, they are Christ's own people, he must certainly be that God to whom the Scriptures assign that people.

99. But the evangelist commends to every thoughtful person for consideration, what a shame and disgrace it is that the world does not recognize its Creator, and that the Jewish people do not receive their God. In what stronger terms can you reprove the world than by saying that it does not know its Creator? What base wickedness and evil report follow from this fact alone! What good can there be where there is nothing but ignorance, darkness, and blindness? What wickedness where there is no knowledge of God! O woe! What a wicked and frightful thing the world is! The one who knew the world and duly pondered this would fall the deeper into perdition. He could not be happy in this life, of which such evil things are written.

But as many as received him, to them gave he the right to become
children of God, even to them that believed on his name.

100. We see now what kind of a Light that is of which the evangelist has hitherto been speaking. It is Christ, the comforting light of grace, and not the light of nature or reason. For John is an evangelist and not a Platonist. All who receive the light of nature and reason receive him according to that light; how could they receive him otherwise? Just as they receive the natural life from the divine life. However, that light and that life do not give them any power to become the children of God. Yea, they remain the enemies of this Light, do not know it, nor acknowledge it. Therefore, there can be no reference in this Gospel to the light of nature, but only to Christ, that he may be acknowledged as true God.

101. From now on, this Gospel is familiar to all, for it speaks of faith in Christ's name, that it makes us God's children. These are excellent words and powerfully refute the teachers of the law, who preach only good works. Good works never bring about a change of heart. Therefore, although the work righteous are ever changing and think they are improving their deeds, in their hearts they remain the same, and their works only become a mantle for their shame and hypocrisy.

102. But, as has often been said, faith changes the person and makes out of an enemy a child, so mysteriously that the external works, walk, and conversation remain the same as before, when they are not by nature wicked deeds. Therefore, faith brings with it the entire inheritance and highest good of righteousness and salvation, so that these need not be sought in works, as the false teachers of good works would have us believe. For he who is a child of God has already God's inheritance through his sonship. If, then, faith gives this sonship, it is manifest that good works should be done freely, to the honor of God, since they already possess salvation and the inheritance from God through faith. This has been amply explained heretofore in the sermon on the second Epistle for this day.

Who were born, not of blood, nor of the will of the flesh,
nor of the will of man, but of God.

103. To explain himself, the evangelist here tells us what faith does, and that everything is useless without it. Here he not only does not praise nature, light, reason, and whatever is not of faith, but forcibly overthrows each. This sonship is too great and noble to originate from nature or to be required by it.

104. John mentions four different kinds of sonship: one of blood, another of the will of the flesh, a third of the will of man, the fourth of this will of God. It is evident that the sonship of blood is the natural sonship. With this, he refutes the Jews who boasted that they were of the blood of Abraham and

the patriarchs, relying on the passages of Scripture in which God promises the blessing and the inheritance of eternal salvation to the seed of Abraham. Therefore, they claim to be the only true people and children of God. But here he says, there must be more than mere blood, else there is no sonship of God. For Abraham and the patriarchs received the inheritance, not for blood's sake but for faith's sake, as Paul teaches in Hebrews 11:8. If mere blood relationship were sufficient for this sonship, then Judas the betrayer, Caiaphas, Ananias, and all the wicked Jews who in times past were condemned in the wilderness, would have a proper right to this inheritance. For they were all of the blood of the patriarchs. Therefore, it is said, they were born "not of blood, but of God."

105. The other two relationships, or sonships, to wit, "of the will of the flesh" and "of the will of man," I do not yet sufficiently understand myself. But I see very well that the evangelist thereby wishes to reject everything which is of nature and which nature can accomplish, and that he would retain the birth by God alone. Therefore, there is no danger in whatever manner we explain these two parts and variously attribute them to nature outside of grace. It is all the same. Some understand the sonship of the will of the flesh to come not of blood, but through the law of Moses. He commanded that the nearest kin to the wife of a deceased husband marry the widow, and raise a name and heir to the deceased one, that the name of his friend be not put out of Israel. To this interpretation belongs also the "step" relationship, which comes of the will of the flesh, and not of blood relationship.

106. But the evangelist here calls by the name of flesh man, as he lives in the flesh, which is the common scriptural designation. Therefore, the meaning is, not as men have children outside of their own line of descent, which is carnal and human, and takes place in accordance with man's free will, but what is born in the line of ancestral blood, takes place without the free will, according to nature, whether a man wills it or not.

107. The third kind of sonship mentioned is "of the will of man." This is taken to mean the sonship of strangers, commonly called "adoption," as when a man chooses and adopts a strange child as his own. Though you were Abraham's or David's real child, or stepchild, or you had been adopted, or you were a stranger, it would all be of no benefit to you unless you were born of God. Even Christ's own friends and relatives did not believe in him, as we are told, in John 7:5.

108. But those who wish may explain this relationship as follows: "Those born of blood" may mean all those who belong to the blood relationship, whether it be a full or a step relationship; "those born of the will of the flesh" may include all those who are not born of blood, or those who have been

adopted into the relationship. But "those who are born of the will of man" are spiritual children of those who are the disciples or followers of a teacher. Thus the evangelist rejects everything that might be accomplished by blood, flesh, nature, reason, art, doctrine, law, free will, with all their powers, so that no one may presume to help another by means of his own doctrine, work, art, or free will, or be allowed to help any man upon earth to the kingdom of God; he is to reject everything, except the striving after the divine birth.

I am also inclined to think that "man" in the Scriptures usually means a superior, who rules, leads, and teaches others. These are properly and before all others rejected, since no relationship is more stubborn, more insolently presumptuous, and confides more in itself than this, and does most strenuously oppose grace at all times, and persecutes the Lord of grace. In this respect, let everyone have his opinion, as long as he bears in mind that nothing avails which is not born of God. For if something else would have availed anything, the evangelist would without doubt have put it side by side with the divine birth, especially as he looks for it so carefully, and would not have exalted only this divine birth.

109. The divine birth is, therefore, nothing else than faith. How can this be? It has been explained above how the light of grace opposes and blinds the light of reason. If now the Gospel comes and bears witness to the light of grace, that man must not live and do according to his fancy, but must reject, put away, and destroy the light of nature, if this man accepts and follows such testimony, gives up his own light and fancy, is willing to become a fool, allows himself to be led, taught, and enlightened, he will be entirely changed, that is, in his natural light. His old light is extinguished and a new light, to wit, faith, is kindled. He follows this new light in life and in death, clings solely to the witness of John or the Gospel, even should he be compelled to abandon all he had and could do before.

Behold, he is now born again of God through the Gospel, in which he remains, and lets go his own light and fancy, as Saint Paul says, "For in Christ Jesus I begat you through the Gospel," in 1 Corinthians 4:15; again, "Of his own will he brought us forth by the word of truth, that we should be a kind of first fruits of his creatures," in James 1:18. Therefore, Saint Peter calls us "new born babes," in 1 Peter 2:2. It is for this reason also that the Gospel is called the womb of God, in which we are conceived, carried, and born as a woman conceives, carries, and bears a child in her womb. Isaiah says, "Hearken unto me, O house of Jacob, and all the remnant of the house of Israel, that have been borne by me from their birth, that have been carried from the womb," in Isaiah 46:3.

110. But this birth properly shows its power in times of temptation and death. There it becomes evident who is born again, and who is not. Then the old light, reason, struggles and wrestles and is loath to leave its fancies and desires, is unwilling to consider and resort to the Gospel, and let go its own light. But those who are born again, or are then being born again, spend their lives in peace and obedience to the Gospel, confide in and cling to the witness of John, and let go their light, life, property, honor, and all they have. Therefore, they come to the eternal inheritance as real children.

111. But when this light, reason, and man's old conceit are dead, dark, and changed into a new light, then the life and all powers of man must be changed and be obedient to the new Light. For where the will goes, reason follows, and love and pleasures follow the will. And so the whole man must be hid in the Gospel, become a new creature, and put off the old Adam, as the serpent puts off its old skin. When the skin becomes old, the serpent seeks a narrow crevice in the rock, crawls through it, sheds its old skin, and leaves it on the outside.

Thus man must resort to the Gospel and to God's Word, confidently trusting their promises, which never fail. In this way, he puts off the old Adam, sets aside his own light and conceit, his will, love, desire, speech, and his deeds, and becomes an entirely new man, who sees everything in a different manner than before, judges differently, thinks differently, wills differently, speaks and loves and desires differently, acts and conducts himself differently than he did before. He now understands whether all the conditions and works of men are right or wrong, as Saint Paul says, "He that is spiritual judgeth all things, and he himself is judged of no man," in 1 Corinthians 2:15.

112. He now sees clearly what great fools they are who pretend to become pious through their good works. He would not give one farthing for all the preachers, monks, popes, bishops, tonsures, cowls, incense, illuminations, burning of candles, singing, organs, prayers, with all their external performances; for he sees how all this is simple idolatry, and foolish dissimulation, just as the Jews prayed to Baal, Ashtaroth, and the calf in the wilderness, which they looked upon as precious things in the old light of stubborn, self-conceited reason.

113. From this, it is evident that no blood, nor relationship, nor command, nor doctrine, nor reason, nor free will, nor good works, nor exemplary living, nor Carthusian orders, nor any religious orders, though they were angelic, are of any use or help to this sonship of God; but they are only a hindrance. For where reason is not first renewed and in agreement with the new birth, it takes offense, becomes hardened and blinded, so that it will scarcely, if ever, be able to be righted; but thinks its doings and ways are right and proper,

storming and raving against all who disregard and reject its doings. Therefore, the old man remains the enemy of God and of grace, of Christ and of his light, beheads John and destroys his testimony, the Gospel, and sets up his own human doctrines. Thus the game goes on even now, in full splendor and power, in the doings of the pope and his clergy, who together know nothing of this divine birth. They prattle and speak nonsense in their doctrines and commandments of certain good works, with which they hope to attain grace, though still clad in the old Adam.

114. But what is here said remains unchangeable: Not of blood, not of the will of the flesh nor of man, but of God, is this new birth. We must despair of our own will, works, and life, which have been poisoned by the false, stubborn, selfish light of reason; in all things, listen to the voice and testimony of the Baptist; believe and obey it. Then the true Light, Christ, will enlighten us, renew us, and give us power to become the sons of God. For this reason, he came and was made man, as follows:

III. CHRIST'S INCARNATION

And the Word became flesh, and dwelt among us, (and we beheld his glory, glory as of the only begotten from the Father,) full of grace and truth.

115. By "flesh" we understand the whole man, body and soul, according to the Scriptures, which call man "flesh," as above, when it is said, "Not of the will of the flesh"; and in the creed we say, "I believe in the resurrection of the body" (German: flesh), that is, of all men. Again Christ says, "Except those days had been shortened, there would be no flesh saved," that is, no man, in Matthew 24:22. Again, "He remembered that they were but flesh, a wind that passeth away, and cometh not again," in Psalm 78:39. Again, "Thou gavest him authority over all flesh, that to all whom thou hast given him, he should give eternal life," in John 17:2.

116. I speak of this the more fully because this passage has occasioned so much offense on the part of heretics at the time when there were learned and great bishops. Some, as Photinus and Appollinaris, taught that Christ was a man without a soul, and that the divine nature took the place of the soul in him. Manichaeus taught that Christ did not have true, natural flesh, but was only an apparition, passing through his mother, Mary, without assuming her flesh and blood, just as the sun shines through a glass, but does not assume its nature. In opposition to all these, the evangelist uses a comprehensive word and says, "He became flesh," that is, a man like every other man, who has flesh and blood, body and soul.

117. Thus the Scriptures, one part after another, had to be tried and confirmed, until the time of the Antichrist, who suppressed them not in parts, but in their entirety. For it has been prophesied that at the time of Antichrist all heresy should be united into one parasitic whole and devour the world. This could not have happened at a better time than when the pope set aside the whole Scriptures, and in their place set up his own law. Therefore, bishops are now no more heretics, nor can they become heretics; for they have no part of the book by which heretics are made, to wit, the Gospel. They have piled up all heresy within and among themselves.

118. In times past, heretics, however bad they were, still remained in the Scriptures, and left some parts intact. But what is left since this divine birth and faith are no more acknowledged and preached, and in their stead only human law and works? What matters it, whether Christ is God or not God, whether he was flesh or a mere apparition, whether he had a soul or not, whether he had come before or after his mother, or whether all error and heresy which have ever been, would prevail? We would have no more of him than all those heretics and do not need him. He seems to have become man in vain, and all things written about him seem to be to no purpose, because we have ourselves found a way by which we may by our own works come to the grace of God!

119. Therefore, there is no difference between our bishops and all heretics that have ever lived, except this that we name Christ with our mouth and pen, for the sake of appearance. But among ourselves we speak of him, and are as little benefited by him, as though he were one with whom all heretics might play the fool. Thus Saint Peter has prophesied and said, "These shall be false teachers among you, who shall privily bring in destructive heresies, denying even the Master that bought them," in 2 Peter 2:1.

120. What does it profit, though Christ be not what the heretics make him, if he is no more to us than to them, and does no more for us? What does it profit to condemn the heretics, and know Christ aright, if we have no different faith in him than they had? I see no reason for the need of Christ, if I am able to attain grace by my works. It is not necessary for him to be God and man. In short, all that is written about him is unnecessary; it would be sufficient to preach God alone, as the Jews believe, and then obtain his grace by means of my works. What more would I want? What more would I need?

121. Christ and the Scriptures are not necessary, as long as the doctrine of the pope and his schools exist. Therefore, I have said that pope, bishops, and schools are not good enough to be heretics; but they surpass all heretics, and are the dregs of all heresies, errors, and idolatry from the beginning,

because they entirely suppress Christ and the Word of God, and only retain their names for appearance's sake. This no idolater, no heretic, no Jew has ever done, not even the Turk [Muslim] with all his violent acts. And although the heathen were without the Scriptures and without Christ before his birth, yet they did not oppose him and the Scriptures, as these do. Therefore, they were far better than the papists.

122. Let us be wise in these times in which Antichrist is powerful, and let us cling to the Gospel, which does not teach us that reason is our light, as men teach us, but which presents Christ as indispensable to our salvation, and says, The Word, by which all things were made, is life, and the life is the light of men. Firmly believe that Christ is the Light of men, that without him all is darkness in man, so that he is unable to know what to do or how to act, to say nothing about being able to attain the grace of God by his own works, as the foolish schools with their idol, the pope, teach and deceive all the world.

123. He came that he might become the Light of men, that is, that he might become known; he showed himself bodily and personally among men and was made man. He is the light on the candlestick. The lost piece of money did not of itself and with light in hand go after and seek the lighted candle, but the candle with its light sought the piece of money and found it; it has swept the house of this whole world in every nook and corner with its broom; and it continues to seek, sweep, and find even until the last day.

124. But that the Word and not the Father was made flesh, and that both are one complete, true God, is a great mystery. Yet faith apprehends it all, and it is proper that reason should not apprehend it; it happened and is written that reason should not apprehend it, but become altogether blind, dazzled, and stupefied, changing from its old false light into the new light.

125. Yet this article is not opposed to the light of reason, which says that we must serve God, believe, and be pious, which accords with this article. But if reason is called on to say exactly who this God is, it is startled and says, "This is not God," and so makes a God according to its fancy. Therefore, when it is informed that this Word is God and that the Father is the same God, it doubts, hesitates, and imagines the article to be wrong and untrue, continues in its conceit and fancy, and thinks it knows better what God is and who he is than anyone else.

126. Thus the Jews continue in their opinion, and do not doubt at all that God is to be believed and honored; but who this God is, they explain according to their own fancy, claim to be masters themselves, and even make God a liar. See then, thus reason does to all of God's works and words, continues to cry that God's work and Word are to be honored, but claims that it is its

privilege and judgment to say what is God's work and Word. It would judge God in all his works and words, but is unwilling to be judged by him. What God is or is not, must be according to its caprice.

127. Consider whether God does not justly express his anger in the Scriptures against such immeasurable wickedness, whether he does not rightly prefer open sinners to such saints. What would you think more vexatious than such wicked presumptuousness? I say this that we may recognize the delicious fruit to which the pope and his schools attribute so much, and which of itself and by its own exertions, without Christ, provides the grace of God. They are God's greatest enemies, and would annihilate him, in order that they might be God themselves, and succeed in making men believe that the grace of God is obtained as they prescribe. This surely is real darkness.

128. See, in this way reason must make idols, and cannot do otherwise; it knows very well how to talk of God's honor, but goes and bestows the same honor on him whom it fancies to be God. Such a one is certainly not God, but is reason's fancy and error, of which the prophets in various ways complained. Nor does it improve the matter, if anyone were to say, as the Jews do, "Yes, I mean the God who has created the heavens and the earth; here I cannot be mistaken, and must be right." In Isaiah 48:1, God himself answers, "Hear ye this, who swear by the name of Jehovah, and make mention of the God of Israel, but not in truth, nor in righteousness." And Jeremiah 5:2 says, "And though they say, as Jehovah liveth; surely they swear falsely."

129. How is this to be accounted for? It happens thus that he who does not accept God in the particular manner in which God has revealed himself, will profit nothing, if he afterward accepts God in the manner which he has selected for himself. If Abraham had said that it was neither God nor God's work that commanded him to sacrifice his son Isaac, but would have followed his reason and have said he would not sacrifice his son, but would serve the God who made heaven and earth in some other way, what would it have profited him? He would have lied; for he would in that very thing have rejected the God who created the heavens and the earth, and would have devised another God, under the name of the God who had created the heavens and the earth, and would have despised the true God, who had given him the command.

130. Behold, thus they all lie who say, they mean the true God who created the heavens and the earth, and yet do not accept his work and Word, but exalt their own opinion above God and his Word. If we truly believed in the God who had created heaven and earth, they would also know that the same God is a creator of their imagination, makes, breaks, and judges it as he

pleases. But as they do not allow him to be a creator of themselves and their fancies even in a small degree, it cannot be true that they believe him to be the creator of all creation.

131. Perhaps you will say, What if I were deceived, and he were not God? Answer: Do not worry, dear soul; a heart that does not trust in its own fancy God will not allow to be deceived; for it is not possible that he should not enter such a heart and dwell there. Mary says, "He hath filled the hungry with good things," in Luke 1:53. The psalmist says, "He satisfieth the longing soul," in Psalm 107:9. But if any is deceived, it is certain that he trusted in his own fancy, either secretly or openly. Therefore a hungry soul always stands in fear in those things that are uncertain, whether they be of God. But self-conceited persons are immediately taken with them, thinking it sufficient if the things glitter and take their fancy. Again, what is certain to be of God, the simple accept at once, but the arrogant persecute it.

132. Now there is no surer sign of a thing of God than that it is against or beyond our fancy. Likewise the arrogant think, there is no surer sign that a thing is not of God than that it is against their fancy. For they are makers and masters of God, and so make those things God and of God which accord with their fancy. Therefore, all those who depend upon themselves must be deceived, and all those who are simple-minded, and not preoccupied with themselves, are safe; they are they who keep the true Sabbath. Where this fancy goes so far as to employ the Word of God in defense of its arrogance and to apply the Scriptures according to its own light, there is neither hope nor help. Such people think the Word of God on their side, and they must safeguard it. This is the last fall, and is the real mischief of Lucifer, of whom Solomon speaks, "A righteous man falleth seven times, and riseth up again; but the wicked are overthrown by calamity," in Proverbs 24:16.

133. Of this, there is now enough; let us come back again to the Gospel. John says, "And the Word became flesh, and dwelt among us"; that is, he lived among men upon earth, as other men do. Even though he was God, he became a citizen of Nazareth and Capernaum, and conducted himself as other men did. Thus Saint Paul says, "Who, existing in the form of God, counted not the being man equality with a thing to be grasped, but emptied himself, taking the form of a servant, being made in the likeness of men; and being found in fashion as a man, he humbled himself, becoming obedient even unto death, yea, the death of the cross," in Philippians. 2:6–8.

134. Now this "likeness" and "dwelling" of Christ must not be understood of his human nature, in which he has been made like unto men. But these words must be understood as referring to his external being and mode of

living such as eating, drinking, sleeping, walking, working, resting, hearth and home, and standing, and all human conduct and deportment, by which no one could recognize him as God, had he not been so proclaimed by John in the Gospel.

IV. THE REVELATION OF CHRIST'S GLORY

135. He says further, "We behold his glory," that is, his divinity through his miracles and teachings. The word "glory" we have heard before in the Epistle, where it was said of Christ, that Christ is the "brightness of the Father's glory," which means his divinity. Our word "glory" comes from the Latin *"gloria."* The corresponding word in Hebrew is *"kabod"* and the Greek word is *"doxa."* Thus we speak of a ruler or a great man having achieved an accomplishment with great glory, and that everything passed off gloriously, when it has passed off well, successfully, and bravely.

Glory does not only mean a great repute, or far-famed honor, but it means also the things which give occasion for the fame, such as costly houses, vessels, clothes, servants, and the like, as Christ says of Solomon, "Consider the lilies of the field, how they grow; they toil not, neither do they spin; yet I say unto you, that even Solomon in all his glory was not arrayed like one of these," in Matthew 6:28–29. In the book of Esther, we read, "King Ahasuerus made a great feast . . . when he showed the riches of his glorious kingdom," in Esther 1:3–4. Thus we say, This is a glorious thing, a glorious manner, a glorious deed, *"gloriosa res."* This is also what the evangelist means when he says, "We have seen his glory," to wit, his glorious being and deeds, which are not an insignificant, common glory, but the glory as of the only begotten of the Father.

136. Here he expresses who the Word is, of whom he and Moses have been speaking, namely, the only begotten Son of God, who has all the glory of the Father. He calls him the only begotten, so as to distinguish him from all the children of God, who are not natural children as this one is. With these words is shown his true divinity; for if he were not God, he could not in preference to others be called the only begotten Son, which is to say that he and no other is the Son of God. This cannot be said of angels and pious men. For not one of them is the Son of God, but are all brethren and creatures of a like creation, children elected by grace, and not children born out of God's nature.

137. But the expression, "We beheld his glory," does not refer only to bodily sight; for the Jews also saw his glory, but did not regard it as the glory of the only begotten Son of God: it refers to the sight of the faithful, who believe it in their hearts. Unbelievers, who beheld only the worldly glory, did not

notice this divine glory. Nor can these two tolerate each other. He that would be glorious before the world for God's sake, will be glorious before God.

Full of grace and truth.

138. These two words are commonly used together in the Scriptures. "Grace" means that whatsoever Christ does is ever pleasing and right. Furthermore, in man there is only disfavor and guile; all that he does is displeasing to God. In fact, he is fundamentally untrue and puts on a vain show, as the psalmist says, "All men are liars," in Psalm 116:11. And again, "Surely every man at his best estate is altogether vanity," in Psalm 39:5.

139. This passage is opposed to the presumptuous papists and Pelagians, who find something outside of Christ, which they claim is good and true; and yet in Christ alone is grace and truth. It is indeed true, as has been said above, that there are some things outside of Christ which are true and pleasing, as the natural light, which teaches that three and two are five, that God should be honored, and the like.

But this light never accomplishes its end; for as soon as reason is to act, and make use of its light, and exercise it, it confuses everything, calls that which is good bad, and that which is bad good; calls that the honor of God which is his dishonor, and vice versa. Therefore, man is only a liar and vain, and unable to make use of this natural light except against God, as we have already said.

140. It is unnecessary to look for the armor in this Gospel; it is all armor and the chief part, upon which is founded the article of faith that Christ is true God and true man, and that without grace, nature, free will, and works are nothing but deception, sin, error, and heresy in spite of papists and Pelagians.

Index by Source

The sermons included in this volume may be found in *the Sermons of Martin Luther: the Church Postils*, collected in volumes 1–4 of *the Complete Sermons of Martin Luther*. Edited by John Nicholas Lenker. Translated by John Nicholas Lenker and others. Published by Baker Books, a division of Baker Book House Company, Grand Rapids, Michigan 49516.

Index by Key Scripture Passage